Original title: Germanic Tribe. Epic Battles

© Germanic Tribe. Epic Battles, Carlos Martínez Cerdá and Víctor Martínez Cerdá, 2025

Authors: Víctor Martínez Cerdá and Carlos Martínez Cerdá (V&C Brothers)

© Cover and illustrations: V&C Brothers

Layout and design: V&C Brothers

All rights reserved.

This publication may not be reproduced, stored, recorded, or transmitted in any form or by any means, whether mechanical, photochemical, electronic, magnetic, electro-optical, by photocopying, or information retrieval systems, or any other current or future method, without prior written permission from the copyright holders.

GERMANIC TRIBE

EPIC BATTLES

INDEX

Germans versus Romans

1. Battle of the Teutoburg Forest (9 AD):
The Cherusci under Arminius annihilate three Roman legions led by General Varus. Major Roman defeat.

2. Battle of Idistaviso (16 AD):
Germanicus defeats the Cherusci led by Arminius.

3. Battle of the Weser River (16 AD):
Part of Germanicus's campaign to avenge Teutoburg.

4. Battle of the Decuman Fields (271 AD):
Emperor Aurelian defeats the Juthungi and Alamanni in northern Italy.

5. Battle of Mediolanum (Milan) (259 AD):
Emperor Gallienus defeats the Alamanni.

6. Battle of the Rhine River (351 AD):
Constantius Gallus fights against the Alamanni.

7. Battle of Argentoratum (Strasbourg) (357 AD):
Emperor Julian defeats the Alamanni, securing the Rhine frontier.

8. Battle of Carnuntum (170 AD):
During the Marcomannic Wars, the Germanic tribes invade Pannonia.

9. Battle of Vindobona (173 AD):
Marcus Aurelius fights against the Marcomanni and Quadi near present-day Vienna.

10. Battle of Aquileia (238 AD):
Roman troops confront Germanic tribes threatening northern Italy.

Battles Between Germanic Tribes

11. War between the Suebi and the Cherusci (1st century AD): Power struggles between tribes following the Roman withdrawal.

12. Battle between the Marcomanni and the Lombards (2nd century BC): Territorial rivalries in Magna Germania.

13. Conflicts between the Vandals and the Visigoths (4th century AD): During the migrations, clashes occurred over control of routes and resources.

14. Battle between the Salian and Ripuarian Franks (3rd century AD): Struggle for supremacy between factions of the same people.

15. Conflict between the Alamanni and the Burgundians (4th century AD): Disputes among Germanic tribes in the Rhine region.

Germans Versus Other Peoples

16. Battle against the Dacians (1st century BC): Germanic tribes allied against the Dacians in the Balkans.

17. Battle against the Celts (Gauls) (1st century BC): Germanic tribes cross the Rhine and invade Celtic territories.

18. Battle against the Sarmatians (2nd century AD): In the Danubian steppes, the Marcomanni and Quadi confront these nomadic horsemen.

19. Clash against the Scythians (3rd century BC): Eastern Germanic tribes come into contact with Scythian tribes around the Black Sea.

20. Battle of the Moselle River (388 AD): The Franks fight against the Huns and other eastern tribes.

Famous Sayings of the Germanic Peoples

- "The forest is our fortress, and our gods are the trees that shelter us." (Germanic tribal maxim)

- "No one fears death when dying fighting alongside their own." (Common saying among the Cherusci)

- "We do not inherit the land from our fathers; we defend it with our blood." (Marcomannic proverb)

- "The German is born free or dies fighting to be so." (Phrase attributed to a Suebi chieftain)

- "He who does not fear the winter does not fear the enemy." (Traditional saying of the Chauci)

- "The Romans build walls; we build men." (Germanic reply recorded by Tacitus)

- "Honor lies at the tip of the spear, not in the words of a foreigner." (Bastarnae proverb)

- "One warrior is worth a hundred slaves." (Tribal motto of the Chatti)

- "The clan forgets neither the traitor nor the one who dies fighting." (Maxim of the Tencteri)

- "Our laws are simple: do not flee, do not kneel, do not forget." (Saying among the Hermunduri)

- "The forest makes us invisible, the storm makes us unstoppable." (Warrior phrase of the Bructeri)

- "He who looks back in battle is already dead." (Motto of the Sicambri)

- "The shield is my father, the spear my brother."

(Proverb among young warriors)

- "The gods smile upon the one who dies with head held high and arm outstretched." (Germanic funerary saying)

- "Freedom is not negotiated; it is conquered." (Phrase attributed to a Quadi king)

- "The Romans offer coins, but demand our soul." (Common maxim in tribal assemblies)

- "I would rather be a wolf in the forest than a slave in the city." (Popular saying among the Suebi)

- "Our dead live in every tree and every river." (Ancient Germanic saying)

- "The thunder of the storm is nothing compared to the roar of a Germanic army." (War phrase attributed to a Marcomannic chieftain)

- "The land is ours as long as we have the strength to defend it." (Proverb of the Lombards)

- "Rome's promises are like frost: beautiful, but they vanish in the sun." (Germanic saying recorded by Roman chroniclers)

- "The warrior who fears death does not deserve to carry a shield." (Initiation motto among young Chauci warriors)

- "Our gods are not found in temples, but in the roar of the forest." (Tribal proverb)

- "Rome fears those it cannot buy." (Saying of the Chatti, according to Tacitus)

- "The iron of the spear is cold, but blood is warm." (Saying among the Tencteri)

- "Men die, but the name of the clan must not perish." (Germanic maxim)

- "The first step toward slavery is accepting peace with the enemy." (Radical phrase of the Cherusci)

- "The raven sings for the fallen, the clan sings for the brave." (Funerary saying)

- "The forest does not betray men do." (Ancient Germanic maxim)

- "Today we fight so that tomorrow our children may walk free upon this land." (Common phrase before battle, recorded by Roman chroniclers)

- "Our strength is not born of numbers, but of the courage burning in every chest." (War cry among the Rugii)

- "Fire consumes the flesh; the clan's song preserves the name." (Germanic funerary proverb)

- "A German does not ask for pay he asks for glory." (Maxim repeated in tribal councils)

- "The axe that sleeps in its sheath is dead weight." (Warning phrase among the Marcomanni)

- "When the raven flies over our dead, let it sing their name, not their shame." (Germanic saying spoken before battle)

- "A German's spear does not bend to promises." (Proverb attributed to the Cherusci)

- "The forest hides us fury reveals us." (Combat phrase among the Chauci)

GERMANIC TRIBES AGAINST ROMANS

1

Battle of the Teutoburg Forest (9 AD)

In the year 9 AD, the Roman Empire was in a phase of expansion into the wild lands beyond the Rhine.

Emperor Augustus had entrusted his general, Publius Quinctilius Varus, with the task of turning the region of Magna Germania into a new province.

Varus was a career politician with little experience in such campaigns, but he believed he commanded an invincible force: three veteran legions — the XVII, XVIII, and XIX — along with auxiliary troops and a retinue of civilians, merchants, and administrative personnel.

His entire force numbered between 20,000 and 25,000 people, of whom at least 15,000 were professional Roman soldiers.

These legionaries were armed with gladius and pilum, and protected by lorica segmentata armor, curved shields, and bronze helmets.

The auxiliary troops included light cavalry, archers, and allied native forces.

There were no siege engines or boats, as the army was marching deep into Germanic territory toward their winter quarters.

The mission was not military, but administrative, and thus the army advanced with confidence, spread out and unprepared for combat.

Among Rome's allies in the region was Arminius, a prince of

the Cherusci tribe, who had been educated in Rome, spoke fluent Latin, and held Roman citizenship and the rank of equestrian.

He knew Roman tactics, discipline, and arrogance inside out and it was precisely that arrogance he exploited to deceive Varus.

Feigning loyalty, Arminius informed him of an alleged rebellion to the north and urged him to march urgently to suppress it.

Varus, unsuspecting, agreed, unaware that Arminius had already secretly united a coalition of Germanic tribes, including the Cherusci, Bructeri, Marsi, and Chatti, with the plan to ambush and annihilate the legions.

The exact number of Germanic warriors is uncertain, but estimates range from 15,000 to 20,000, armed with spears, axes, iron swords, bows, and wooden shields.

They lacked Roman discipline but knew the terrain like the back of their hand and possessed a warrior fury that fueled their shared cause: to drive out the invaders.

The sky was cloaked in ash and rain when the nightmare began.

It was September of the year 9 AD, and the Teutoburg Forest, always damp and silent, whispered a deathly omen through its branches.

The three Roman legions of Publius Quinctilius Varus, accompanied by auxiliary troops and a long convoy of civilians, advanced slowly and heavily along a narrow path, surrounded by hills and ravines, through a sea of endless trees.

The column was a vulnerable beast, stretched out over miles of muddy roads, broken by the storm, lulled by a false peace.

The legionaries, soaked and knee-deep in mud, marched beneath a heavy, gray sky.

Rain fell like invisible spears.

The Roman standards fluttered dimly.

Roman discipline still held, but cracks had begun to show: the column was fragmented, scattered, exposed.

Then the forest roared.

It was as if the trees had awakened.

From the slopes, from the underbrush, from behind every trunk, surged a tide of wild bodies.

They were the Cherusci, Bructeri, Chauci, Tencteri, Marsi, and Chatti, all under a single command: Arminius, the Germanic traitor who had deceived Varus into believing there was peace.

Now, his warriors emerged from the forest like wolves on the hunt, covered in mud, furs, and fury, crying out in unison the ancestral war cry of Germania.

The first javelins and arrows rained down on the Romans like hail.

The surprise was total.

The auxiliaries on the flanks and rear were the first to fall, pierced before they could even draw their gladii.

Panic spread like fire among the civilians and the soldiers at the back of the column.

Some tried to flee into the trees; few were ever seen again.

The legionaries, disciplined but surrounded, tried to form a testudo, but the muddy and uneven ground made it impossible.

Water weighed down their shields, helmets slipped in the mud, and the fog limited visibility to just a few meters.

The sound of Germanic war horns and drums drowned out everything else.

The Roman column began to break apart, isolated into segments unable to support each other.

Varus, mounted on his horse, desperate, tried to regroup his forces, sending messengers from one end to the other, but none reached their destination.

Every clearing was a slaughterhouse, every path a blade.

The first day was a bloodbath.

Night fell over an improvised camp, poorly fortified, built under torrential rain.

The legionaries did not sleep.

The campfires barely burned.

The moans of the wounded were joined by the howls of wolves and the echoes of Germanic warriors, who continued to circle the perimeter like specters.

The second day was even worse.

Every attempt to advance became a maze of ambushes.

The Germans had built hidden palisades along the escape route they knew the Romans would try to follow.

Every tree concealed a trap, every hill unleashed a rain of spears.

The Romans died without seeing who was killing them.

Officers were prime targets.

Communications broke down completely.

The swampy ground swallowed men, horses, and hope.

The third day arrived beneath a black sky and an unrelenting downpour.

What remained of the legions, starving, wounded, and caked in mud, attempted one final push toward an open area where they could form up.

But Arminius was already waiting.

The hillsides were lined with palisades and warriors ready for the final assault.

Like a tide, the Germans descended upon the Roman remnants from all sides.

The battlefield turned into a whirlpool of screams, steel, and desperation.

The last standards were brought down.

The centurions died on their feet, shouting orders no one could obey anymore.

Varus, wounded, desperate, and fully aware of the fate that awaited him, threw himself upon his own sword, along with other officers, to avoid the humiliation of captivity.

The end was absolute: those who tried to surrender were

executed or enslaved, and many legionaries were taken alive to be sacrificed to the gods of the forest.

Some were impaled, others drowned in the swamps as offerings.

The legion standards, the sacred eagle of Rome, were captured and nailed to poles at the entrances of Germanic villages as trophies of ancestral vengeance.

The numbers were apocalyptic: over 15,000 Romans dead, three legions — the XVII, XVIII, and XIX — completely annihilated.

The auxiliaries were massacred, and the civilians dragged off as slaves.

Germanic losses were minimal in comparison: only a few hundred, thanks to their knowledge of the terrain and guerrilla tactics.

Days later, when the news reached Rome, the impact was devastating.

Emperor Augustus, upon hearing the account, locked himself away for days and, according to Suetonius, banged his head against the walls of his palace, crying out: "Varus, give me back my legions!"

The Roman world trembled.

The Rhine frontier was marked forever.

Years later, General Germanicus led punitive campaigns to recover the lost standards and avenge the humiliation, but a full annexation of the territory was never attempted again.

Legions XVII, XVIII, and XIX were never reformed;
their numbers were erased as a symbol of shame.

The victory made Arminius a hero among the Germanic peoples, though he would soon face internal betrayals and die at the hands of his own allies.

But his legacy was forever marked: he was the man who stopped the advance of the most powerful empire in the world through cunning, knowledge, and tribal fire.

The Teutoburg Forest was etched into history as one of Rome's greatest military disasters, the place where three legions were lost forever in the mist, the blood, and the rain of a land that never wished to be conquered.

2

Battle of Idistaviso (16 AD)

It was the year 16 AD, and the memory of the massacre in the Teutoburg Forest still hung over Rome like a dark shadow.

The loss of Legions XVII, XVIII, and XIX at the hands of the Germanic tribes led by Arminius had left an open wound in the pride of the Empire.

For Augustus, the affront had been unbearable, but it would be his successor, Emperor Tiberius, who entrusted Germanicus Julius Caesar,a brilliant, charismatic young general and Tiberius's nephewnwith the mission of avenging the defeat, punishing the treacherous tribes, and, if possible, recovering the lost standards.

Thus, over several years, Germanicus launched a fierce and methodical campaign into the heart of Germania, pushing ever deeper beyond the Rhine, razing villages, burning forests, and forging alliances with tribes hostile to Arminius.

It was in this context of blood, resentment, and revenge that the Battle of Idistaviso erupted.

The Roman army deployed by Germanicus was colossal by the standards of the time: six full legions, approximately 30,000 legionaries, supported by 5,000 cavalrymen and around 8,000 auxiliary troops, including Syrian archers, Balearic slingers, Gallic light infantry, and allied Germanic forces such as the Batavi.

Germanicus, as part of his strategy, had also employed a fleet of over 1,000 ships built at the mouth of the Rhine, with which he transported part of the army and supplies through the North Sea and navigable rivers into the Germanic interior.

No large siege engines were used in this battle, as it was a pitched field confrontation.

Germanicus was accompanied by veteran generals such as Aulus Caecina, Gaius Silius, and the camp prefect himself, all maintaining high discipline and morale after years of systematically punishing the hostile tribes.

On the other side, Arminius had managed to regroup his forces after several years of Roman harassment.

Although some tribes had abandoned him or rivaled him for power, he still retained a core of loyal Cheruscan warriors, along with Bructeri and Marsi allies.

His army numbered around 35,000 men, but most were tribal militiamen, poorly equipped and lacking the tactical cohesion of the Roman army.

Nevertheless, they knew the terrain, were fast, fierce, and driven by a desire for freedom and hatred of the invader.

Arminius personally commanded the defense of Idistaviso, a plain flanked by the Weser River to the west and forested hills to the east.

His plan was to use the elevation changes to launch a flanking attack from the woods.

Germanicus, anticipating an ambush, had positioned his troops with meticulous precision.

The battle began at dawn.

The sun had barely begun to rise on the horizon when the Roman drums thundered through the mist of the Weser plain.

The ground was damp, covered in dew, and the silence of dawn hung heavy like an omen.

Across the valley, arrayed in perfect formation, marched Germanicus's army: a disciplined war machine, forged in decades of blood and hardened by the pain of the Teutoburg massacre.

The legions advanced in tight order, their standards proudly fluttering in the breeze.

At the center, the legionary cohorts—the elite of Rome—formed an impenetrable wall of shields and spears, accompanied by their eagles, standards that would not be taken so easily again.

On the flanks, Illyrian, Batavian, and Gallic auxiliary troops marched with steady steps, and behind them, in reserve, the cavalry

Gleaming in the morning light, they awaited the signal from their general to unleash the storm.

And then, the forest roared, for from the hills and slopes, the Germans descended like an avalanche of flesh and fury.

Their war cries tore through the fog, and javelins flew like swarms of steel.

They were thousands, warriors of free clans: Cherusci, Chauci, Marsi, and Bructeri.

Among them, moving like the alpha wolf of the pack, was Arminius, the traitor, the liberator, the scourge of Rome, with his hair wild, face painted, and sword raised high.

At his side was his uncle Inguiomer, an old warrior, fighting to keep their homeland from kneeling before the Roman eagle.

The first Germanic charge was a wall of stone, attempting to crush the discipline of Rome.

Stones and javelins slammed into shields, the voices of the Germans trembling in the wind.

But the Roman line did not break.

Like a cliff resisting a storm, the legionaries dug in their shields and advanced step by step, with surgical precision, answering every blow, every spear, with a rain of iron.

Germanicus, always visible, always present, mounted at the front, raised his sword and, with a fiery cry, ordered the first major maneuver.

The cavalry on the left wing, led by the Batavi and Gauls, thundered down onto the Germanic flank.

The impact was devastating: men and horses clashing like hammers, spears snapping, bodies hurled and crushed beneath hooves.

The Germanic flank, still disorganized from descending the hills, began to fall back.

At the center, the Germanic infantry, savage and numerous, collided head-on with the legions.

The Cherusci shouted the names of their clans, hurling axes and crashing forward with wooden shields.

But the Romans, with unshakable discipline, began to cut through, slashing, pushing, driving their gladii into bellies, necks, and flanks.

The Batavi, fighting as auxiliaries of Rome, recognized among the enemy their own kin relatives and blood brothers.

The battle, already fierce, turned into a personal and ancestral slaughter.

As the morning wore on, Germanicus watched with a hawk's eye the weakening of the Germanic right flank.

He didn't hesitate, he gave the signal, and the cavalry under Aulus Caecina advanced in wedge formation, gleaming like an iron spear hurled from the sky.

The charge was devastating: the Germans began to lose formation, their lines broke, and retreat turned into rout.

Arminius tried to rally his men, appearing everywhere like a demon, fighting hand to hand, urging his warriors on with blood running down his sword and face, but even he realized the tide had turned.

Germanicus showed no mercy, and at the exact moment, he unleashed his Balearic slingers and Syrian archers.

From the rear, a storm of lead and arrows rained down on the fleeing Germans.

The fugitives fell one after another, as the projectiles pierced backs, legs, and throats.

The Germanic retreat became pure panic, and the Romans surged across the plain like a wave of death.

The cavalry followed close behind, slashing down stragglers, trampling the fallen.

Many Germans tried to reach the Weser River to escape, but their bodies were struck down by arrows, or they drowned under the weight of their weapons and the raging current.

Arminius, covered in blood, was wounded in the face by a Roman pilum, a scar he would carry until his death.

Only the bravery of his personal cavalry saved him.

His uncle Inguiomer was not so fortunate: surrounded, he fought like a trapped wolf, cutting down enemies until a gladius pierced him.

When the last cry faded, the plain was carpeted with bodies.

Over 15,000 Germans lay dead or floated in the river.

Thousands more were taken prisoner.

The legions had lost around 800 to 1,000 men, mostly among the auxiliaries who had borne the brunt of the first assault.

Germanicus, calm and victorious, raised a trophy on the battlefield, built from the weapons of the fallen and the recovered standards.

It was not just a message to the barbarians, it was a message to Rome and to History.

The legions had returned to the forest, and the blood of Teutoburg had been avenged.

The soldiers cheered.

The Roman eagle once again soared over the wild lands.

And the name of Germanicus echoed throughout the Empire as the man who, in the mist and mud, had restored Rome's honor.

The consequences were profound.

Although Tiberius, jealous of Germanicus's rising prestige, soon recalled him to Rome and canceled any plans to fully conquer Germania, the Empire had shown that it could punish and defeat those who stood against it.

Arminius, though he survived, lost internal support and was

assassinated three years later by members of his own tribe, who feared his ambition.

Rome did not annex Germania, but it permanently established the Rhine as its eastern frontier.

The Battle of Idistaviso was not only the revenge for Teutoburg, it was the reaffirmation of Rome's will to endure, to strike, and, when necessary, to exact blood for blood.

It was also the last great clash between Rome and the free tribes of Germania, and the end of the dream of eastern expansion.

But above all, it was the moment when Germanicus, young and bold, wrote his name alongside the great generals of history in letters of iron and blood.

3

Battle of the Weser River (16 AD)

In the year 16 AD, the campaign of Germanicus Julius Caesar in Germanic lands reached its climax.

Following the bloody Roman victory at Idistaviso, the legions of Rome were still not satisfied: their goal was not only to punish the Cherusci for the betrayal at Teutoburg seven years earlier, but to erase the humiliation suffered by the Empire through the complete annihilation of Arminius's power.

The young and charismatic General Germanicus, nephew and adopted son of Emperor Tiberius, had launched a massive offensive into the heart of Magna Germania, pushing forward with a colossal force across the Rhine, using land, river, and sea routes, and exploiting the rivers as arteries of war.

The campaign became not just a war of blood, but a battle for the soul of the Empire: Rome versus rebellion, discipline against barbarism, order confronting chaos.

Germanicus had organized an extraordinary force: six legions — around 30,000 legionaries — reinforced by nearly 5,000 cavalry and over 8,000 auxiliary troops, including Balearic slingers, Syrian archers, Gallic light infantry, and Batavian cohorts.

The fleet also played a crucial role: more than a thousand vessels of various types, from river galleys to heavy transports, sailed the Rhine and the Weser, carrying supplies, reinforcement troops, and even serving as mobile firing platforms.

Although they did not carry large siege engines, the Romans had engineers capable of constructing palisades, ramps, and fortified camps within a matter of hours.

Command was in the hands of Germanicus, alongside his key generals Aulus Caecina, Gaius Silius, and the praetorian prefect.

The army advanced with relentless pace, leaving behind razed villages and devastated fields, forcing Arminius to face them once again.

On the other side, the Cheruscan leader found himself in a critical situation.

Although he had survived Idistaviso, his forces were diminished, and his prestige had suffered a severe blow.

Nonetheless, he still retained the loyalty of part of his people and had once again assembled a coalition of tribes: Cherusci, Bructeri, Marsi, Chatti, and several smaller Germanic tribes.

His army was numerically comparable to the Roman force —possibly even slightly larger, around 40,000 men—but with serious tactical and organizational weaknesses.

They were mostly tribal warriors, armed with spears, axes, longswords, and wooden or hide-covered shields, without armor or a formal chain of command.

Arminius, however, was a master of irregular warfare and knew the terrain better than any Roman.

He understood that his only hope lay in luring the Romans into a trap, using the mobility of his forces, and taking advantage of every tree, every bend in the river, every patch of mist.

The Battle of the Weser River took place shortly after Idistaviso and was an immediate continuation of Germanicus's pursuit.

After his previous defeat, Arminius had withdrawn further east, seeking a strategic point along the river to make a stand: a place with gentle slopes and forest on one side, and the river on the other.

Germanicus, instead of pulling back to consolidate, pressed forward with all his might.

The battle began with the murmur of scouts, a game of shadows and spears in the days leading up, as Rome's Batavi and Germanic sentinels hunted each other on the forest's edge like wolves and deer.

For days on end, small skirmishes foreshadowed the coming storm.

Both armies knew it was merely the held breath before the scream.

Finally, at dawn on a sunless day, with the sky covered in low clouds and the scent of wet earth in the air, Arminius accepted the challenge and offered battle in open ground.

He knew that his power, his leadership, and the very unity of the tribes depended on a clear victory.

The Cherusci, Bructeri, and Chauci clans formed in disordered lines, trembling with impatience and fury.

Their drums echoed through the trees, and crows circled the plain above, hungry.

Before them, across the open meadow, Germanicus deployed the Roman colossus.

At the center stood a living wall of steel: the legions, disciplined and impenetrable, formed in tight blocks, their standards fluttering like flames above a sea of shields.

On the flanks, auxiliary cohorts: Batavians, Illyrians, Gauls, hardened by years of war.

At the outer edges, Roman and allied cavalry waited like a storm held in check, and farther back, the Balearic slingers and Syrian archers drew their weapons, ready to fill the sky with death.

Germanicus raised his hand, and the whistling of war horns signaled the beginning.

A rain of projectiles fell upon the front Germanic lines.

Stones, bolts, and arrows tore through air and flesh, cutting down dozens of warriors before they could charge, but the Germans did not stop.

Like a wave of primal fury, shouting the names of their clans, pounding shields with axes and spears, they began to advance in uneven waves.

From a rise, Arminius watched, his silhouette stark against the gray sky.

His hair hung loose, his eyes ablaze.

He knew he could not match Roman discipline, so he sought maneuver: from the forests on both flanks, he attempted to execute a pincer movement, sending groups of light warriors to encircle the Roman formation.

But Germanicus had read the game before it began.

With a swift gesture, he ordered his auxiliary cohorts and light cavalry to move into the woods, striking before they could be struck.

The Germans were caught mid-maneuver, their ranks scattered among the trees, and there began the silent slaughter, hand-to-hand, far from the center of the plain.

Meanwhile, at the heart of the battle, the Roman center held firm like a cliff beneath a storm.

The legions advanced step by step, hurling their pilum at first contact, then drawing their gladius to carve a path forward.

The Germans charged again and again, but crashed into a wall of steel.

The Batavians on the flanks fought with brutal ferocity, familiar with the terrain, many with Germanic blood in their veins and rage in their hearts.

At a critical moment, when the Roman left flank seemed to waver, Arminius saw his chance.

At the head of his personal guard, he descended the hill like lightning, leading a fierce charge, aiming to break the line and split the enemy in two.

But Germanicus, ever watchful, unleashed Silius's heavy cavalry, which burst forth like thunder upon the Germanic charge.

The collision was brutal: horses colliding, spears splintering, men thrown down and trampled.

In the midst of the chaos, Arminius was surrounded.

He fought like a demon, cutting down enemies to his left and right, but a spear strike wounded his arm, and he barely managed to escape, covered in blood, saved by the last riders of his escort.

From that moment on, the battle broke apart.

The Germanic center began to fall back.

The pressure of the legions was unstoppable, like a current of iron.

The tribal warriors, lacking cohesion, began to fall into disarray.

Some tried to flee into the forest, others toward the Weser River, which snaked along the edge of the plain like a liquid wall that promised salvation.

But there, the final trap awaited.

The Roman fleet, deployed along the river, cut off the retreat.

Their ships launched projectiles from the water, cutting down those trying to cross.

The vessels intercepted the few who reached the far shore.

Archers and slingers, advancing to the riverbank, fired mercilessly at the fleeing men.

The entire plain became a slaughterhouse.

The Germans, trapped between the legions, the forest, and the river, fell by the thousands.

Bodies carpeted the field, and the waters of the Weser ran red.

The roar of the slaughter echoed until nightfall.

Germanicus allowed his troops to pursue the stragglers well into the night.

The dying cries mingled with the crack of branches, the river carrying corpses like a funeral procession.

At dawn, when the sun rose over a field strewn with bodies

and broken weapons, Germanicus gathered his men and, in the middle of the plain, ordered an altar of stone and wood to be erected.

There, among the remains of fallen enemies, he honored the legions that had been annihilated years earlier in Teutoburg.

His gesture was clear: vengeance had been fulfilled, for the numbers were overwhelming.

More than 15,000 Germans dead, hundreds taken prisoner, the tribal coalition shattered.

Roman losses, though felt, were minimal in comparison: between 1,000 and 1,500 men fallen, most of them auxiliaries and cavalry on the flanks.

Arminius, wounded and defeated, fled into the forest with the few who had escaped.

His authority was severely damaged.

Many of his allies abandoned him, and within a few years, he would be assassinated by his own kin, victim of internal betrayal.

For Rome, the victory at the Weser was confirmation of its moral and military dominance.

Germanicus had avenged the disaster of Teutoburg with honor and blood.

He had recovered the standards, cleansed the cursed ground, and shattered the myth of Arminius's invincibility.

Yet, paradoxically, it also marked the end of the offensive: Tiberius, fearful of his nephew's growing prestige and the high economic cost of waging a war with no clear end, summoned him back to Rome.

Germanicus returned in glory, celebrated by the people, though he would die mysteriously not long after, under circumstances still clouded by suspicions of poisoning.

The Battle of the Weser was more than just a clash: it was the final echo of a struggle between civilizations, the last roar of Rome in the wild forests of Germania.

It was a victory steeped in honor, vengeance, and politics, where the lost standards flew once more, and where the fury of the Empire finally triumphed over betrayal.

4

Battle of the Decuman Fields (271 AD)

In the year 271 AD, the Roman Empire was going through one of its darkest periods.

The so-called "Crisis of the Third Century" had torn it apart from within and without for decades: emperors who lasted only months, internal rebellions, inflation, plague, and above all, constant invasions by barbarian peoples crossing the weakened frontiers of the Rhine and the Danube.

One of these peoples was the Juthungi, a Germanic tribe related to the Alamanni, who, taking advantage of the Empire's instability, had invaded northern Italy in a devastating campaign.

They sacked cities such as Placentia (modern-day Piacenza), defeated local armies, and even threatened to march on Rome itself.

But in that critical moment, a figure of steel emerged: Lucius Domitius Aurelianus, a general hardened by war, proclaimed emperor by his troops and determined to restore the Empire's lost glory with an iron fist and an unwavering sword.

Aurelian wasted no time in assembling a field army to face the Germanic threat.

The Roman force was composed of a mix of regular troops, vexillationes from various legions of the Danube and Rhine, auxiliary units, and detachments of heavy cavalry from the eastern clibanarii.

It is estimated that Aurelian commanded around 30,000 to 35,000 men, divided into heavy legionary infantry (approximately 20,000), mobile auxiliary troops (about 5,000), eastern archers (2,000), light reconnaissance cavalry (1,500), and around 6,000 heavy cavalry, including cataphracts and clibanarii, armed with long lances, segmented armor, and closed helmets.

The army included engineering units, but no siege engines or ships were employed, as the campaign took place on land in the plains of northern Italy, in the region between the Po River and the Apennines, known as the Decuman Fields (campi decumates), a transitional area between the Italian heartland and the Germanic frontier.

The Juthungi and Alamanni, on the other hand, had assembled a formidable horde, not only of warriors but also of women, elders, and children, as many were not a traditional campaign army but an armed migration, intending to settle in Italian lands.

Their total numbers may have exceeded 50,000, of which around 30,000 were fighters: tribal warriors armed with spears, axes, longswords, and oval wooden shields, with minimal body protection, though experienced in ambushes, assaults, and frontal charges.

Their leadership was divided among several clan chiefs, such as Nebigastes and other tribal nobles, but they lacked a unified chain of command.

Their strategy was to use their mobility and numerical superiority to push southward and plunder the wealthiest regions of the Empire.

The battle took place in the wide, flat fields of northern Italy, a terrain favorable both for cavalry charges and the mass deployment of infantry.

Aurelian, the relentless soldier-emperor, had sworn he would never again be caught off guard as he had been at Placentia.

There, the Juthung horde had descended upon his troops in the darkness like wolves on a moonless night, shattering columns, setting tents ablaze, and forcing the proud Roman army into a humiliating retreat.

But this time, there would be no surprises.

This time, the battlefield would be chosen, prepared, and consecrated by the blood of those who dared stand against Rome.

This time, he would strike the blow.

The chosen site was a broad plain between low hills and scattered woods, terrain the enemy had to cross if they wished to advance into the heart of Italy.

Aurelian ordered hidden trenches to be dug, false retreat lines to be laid, and every rise and dip in the ground to be studied.

It was a field of death disguised as open ground.

He positioned his legionary infantry—around 20,000 hardened men, veterans of the Danube wars—in the center, arranged in staggered lines to form a living wall of shields, spears, and *gladii*.

On the flanks, concealed behind hills and in the shadows of the trees, he deployed his secret weapon: the clibanarii, his eastern heavy cavalry, covered in metal plates from their helmets to the hooves of their horses.

In front of them, a swarm of archers and slingers prepared to darken the sky with death.

Behind, the light cavalry—swift, agile, and ruthless—awaited the order to hunt.

And then, like a roar rising from the northern forests,

the Juthungi arrived.

They came in waves, like a river of bodies armed with spears, axes, and longswords.

They were tens of thousands,perhaps thirty thousand in total a mix of warriors and entire families who had sacked villas, devastated fields, and now wanted Italy for themselves.

Swollen with pride from their previous victory, they descended onto the plain, beating their shields, shouting to their gods, laughing at what seemed like a mere line of Romans waiting to die.

From atop a rise, Aurelian raised his hand.

The archers and slingers unleashed hell.

The sky darkened with projectiles.

Arrows hissed like deadly serpents, stones whistled as they shattered bone.

The front ranks of the Juthungi fell in chaos, splashing the ground with blood.

But they did not stop.

Roaring with fury, driven forward by the thousands behind them, the Juthungi charged like a storm of steel.

The ground shook, and the clash was apocalyptic.

The Roman infantry held firm.

Like a fortress of flesh and discipline, their lines withstood the assault.

The pilum pierced through wooden shields, and when the

enemies were close enough, the gladii began to tear into them.

But the Juthungi were no cowards.

Their assault was so brutal that even the great Roman war machine began to crack at moments.

The left wing started to give way.

Some legionaries were pushed back, others became isolated and died surrounded.

For a moment, it seemed the barbarian tide would break the front, but Aurelian, the unyielding, did not hesitate.

At that moment, with the winds of fate blowing in his favor, he gave the order.

From the hills emerged the clibanarii, charging with unrelenting fury and smashing into the enemy.

Clad in metal, gleaming in the sun like a legion of living statues, they launched their charge against the Juthungi right flank.

It was like the collision of two worlds.

The horses, trained to strike without slowing, crashed into the enemy ranks and shattered them instantly, sending men flying through the air.

The sound of breaking bones mixed with the desperate screams of those who knew they would not escape.

At the same time, the light cavalry, emerging from the woods like ravenous predators, fell upon the enemy rear.

They shot, they slashed, they stabbed.

The trap had closed.

The Juthungi were surrounded.

Amid the chaos, the archers and slingers resumed their attack, this time targeting those who fled, those trying to escape across the fields, those who dropped their weapons and begged for mercy.

There was no mercy: Rome had bled, and Aurelian did not forgive.

The battle raged on for hours.

The entire day was a symphony of death.

The mud turned red, the fields became a cemetery, the screams of the dying mingled with the constant roar of the clash.

When the sun began to set, the plain was no longer green but a carpet of barbarian corpses.

Over 20,000 Juthungi lay dead, thousands more had been captured, many of them executed on the spot by order of the emperor.

The few who managed to escape were ruthlessly hunted down by Roman cavalry in the following days.

Some drowned in rivers, others were lost in the forests, and many never returned to their homeland.

Roman losses were significant, a high price for victory: between 3,000 and 5,000 men fallen, especially on the left wing and among the cavalry who had charged with their souls leading the way.

But Rome had roared and triumphed.

Northern Italy was liberated, the plunder recovered, and thousands of citizens rescued from slavery.

The consequences of this victory were profound, and they temporarily restored Roman control over Italy.

Aurelian, strengthened by the triumph, was acclaimed by his troops and granted the title Restitutor Orbis, Restorer of the World.

Realizing that the Rhine frontier was indefensible in its current state, he ordered the strategic withdrawal from the campi decumates and the reinforcement of Rome's walls: the construction of the Aurelian Wall began, a symbol of an Empire that, though battered, was not broken.

The victory sealed the fate of the Juthungi in Italy, forcing them to retreat beyond the Alps.

But it also showed the world that there were still emperors capable of wielding the sword with the same strength as the crown.

Aurelian had become not only a vanquisher of barbarians but a symbol of the rebirth of the Roman spirit, that spirit which, even when all seemed lost, found the strength to resist, to strike back, and to rise again from the ashes.

In the bloodstained fields of northern Italy, Rome had roared once more.

5

Battle of Mediolanum (Milan) (259 AD)

In the year 259 AD, the Roman Empire was in the midst of the Crisis of the Third Century, a period of near-constant chaos in which barbarian tribes repeatedly breached the frontiers, provinces rebelled, the economy collapsed, and emperors fell as quickly as they were elevated by their legions.

Amid this turmoil, the Alamanni, a coalition of fierce and war-hardened Germanic tribes crossed the Rhine limes and surged like a devastating wave into Gaul and then into Italy, sacking villas, destroying undefended cities, and sparking a panic not seen in centuries.

They penetrated deep into northern Italy, something once thought unthinkable, even approaching the gates of Mediolanum modern-day Milan.

Rome, weakened and without an emperor capable of leading an organized defense, seemed doomed.

But then an unexpected figure emerged: Emperor Gallienus, son of Emperor Valerian, who at that time was campaigning against the Persians in the East.

Gallienus, young, a skilled military leader, and one of the few emperors of this era with a vision for reform, acted swiftly.

He assembled an army composed mostly of vexillationes —mobile detachments drawn from frontier legions— reinforced by a cavalry force he himself had restructured and transformed into a fast and deadly weapon.

His total army is estimated at around 10,000 to 15,000 men:

approximately 6,000 veteran legionaries, well-trained and battle-hardened from recent campaigns; around 2,000 auxiliary infantry; about 1,500 archers and slingers; and at least 4,000 cavalrymen, many of them from the new elite units created by Gallienus, equipped with armor, composite bows, and long lances in the Sarmatian style.

There were no ships or siege engines, as this was a rapid-response campaign in open terrain, aimed at intercepting and destroying the invaders before they could escape with their loot.

The Alamanni, for their part, had entered Italy in large numbers, likely around 30,000 people including warriors and non-combatants.

It was less an organized military invasion than an armed migration: a torrent of tribes, clans, and entire families, with wagons, livestock, women, and children, moving as a nomadic body with fighting capability.

Of these, between 15,000 and 20,000 were warriors, armed with longswords, spears, wooden and hide-covered shields, undisciplined, but fierce and brutally courageous.

Their leadership was divided among several independent tribal chiefs who only coordinated when absolutely necessary.

They were camped around Mediolanum, plundering town after town, confident that no Roman force could challenge them.

But Gallienus arrived faster than they expected. Aware of the enemy's numerical advantage, he chose to use surprise as his main weapon.

He organized a rapid advance with his mobile units, marching by night and moving through forests and hills to conceal his approach.

When he neared the Alemannic camp, Gallienus deployed his

army in open terrain, though still partially covered by groves of trees that concealed his cavalry units.

He positioned his heavy infantry at the center, archers behind them, and auxiliary units on the flanks, with the heavy cavalry held in reserve, hidden and ready for a flanking strike.

The battle erupted at dawn, as the mist still clung to the ground like a sheet of spectral smoke and the sun barely tinged the horizon red, a harbinger of the blood soon to be spilled.

The silence of the field was broken by the dull hum of projectiles that began to rain down from the forest like an invisible curse.

Whistling arrows and relentless sling stones fell upon the Alemanni ranks, who were still deploying, unaware and overconfident.

Cries of pain mixed with curses in barbarian tongues as the first warriors fell into the dew-covered grass of early morning.

The Alemannic chieftains, enraged by the ambush, waited no longer.

Raising their axes and spears, they ordered a massive frontal charge, a chaotic and powerful assault like a storm of flesh and steel.

Thousands of tribal warriors began to pour down across the plain, brandishing their weapons and shouting with a fury that seemed torn from the very bowels of the earth.

The ground trembled beneath their feet.

It was a black, deafening tide, as if all of Germania had come to devour Rome in a single bite.

But Rome was not so easily swallowed.

The Roman front line, formed by Gallienus's veteran legionaries and auxiliaries, absorbed the impact with the cold precision of a perfect machine.

Their interlocked shields formed a wall that groaned under the pressure of the charge, but did not break.

Roman spears shot out like fangs, and when the bodies slammed into the wall of iron, the Roman gladius began its deadly dance: short, precise, devastating.

The Alamanni pushed with force, roaring like wild beasts, but they crashed against a rock.

The Roman center shook, wavered, but did not fall.

Gallienus, standing atop a small rise, watched the fury of battle with the eyes of a hawk.

He did not shout, did not hesitate, he waited.

And when he saw the moment—when the Germanic push began to splinter, when the first signs of doubt crept into the enemy lines—he gave the order.

From both flanks of the Roman army, as if Mars himself had unleashed his riders, the imperial cavalry emerged.

On the right, the cataphracts, armored to the face, launched their charge like thunder.

They were riders of steel, their lances as long as trees, their helmets enclosed, their mounts armored.

The ground trembled beneath their charge.

The Alamanni barely had time to raise their shields before the impact shattered them.

From the left, the light cavalry and mounted archers burst out of the forest like ghosts, firing at full gallop and sowing death among the enemy rear.

It was a perfect pincer, a trap closing, and the chaos was total.

The Alamanni, surrounded and with no room to maneuver, began to fall apart.

The center, which had once roared with strength, now screamed in fear.

The Germanic formation shattered like glass under the final hammer blow of the cavalry.

Some tried to form a defensive circle, a desperate wall of shields.

But the Roman archers, relentless, unleashed a second volley directly into them, tearing bloody holes in that last hope.

Others, seized by terror, fled toward the nearby rivers, throwing down their weapons, shoving their own comrades aside.

But the waters, cold and deep, offered no salvation.

Many drowned; others were cut down at the banks.

And then, like the lightning that ends the storm, Gallienus charged at the front with his personal cavalry.

With sword drawn and a voice like thunder, he swept across the field like a mounted lightning bolt.

He pursued, annihilated, and sealed the victory with the sheer force of his presence.

Roman trumpets echoed amid the groans of the defeated.

No quarter was given.

No mercy was shown to anyone.

By the time the sun reached its zenith, the battle was over.

The field was a sea of corpses, fallen Germanic warriors in every posture, dismembered bodies, splintered shields, broken spears.

Roman losses had been heavy—between 1,000 and 1,200 dead or wounded, mostly among the infantry in the center that bore the brunt of the initial assault—but what they had achieved was the total annihilation of the enemy.

Over 15,000 Alamanni were killed in battle or during the pursuit, and thousands more were captured and chained.

The tribal leaders fell in combat or were executed on the field.

The Germanic threat to Italy had been completely dismantled.

Gallienus had not only saved Mediolanum.

He had wiped an invading army off the map, restored confidence in Rome, and proven that even in times of crisis, the fury of Rome could still set the world ablaze.

The victory was decisive, overwhelming, immortal.

From that day forward, the name of Gallienus was no longer seen merely as the son of Emperor Valerian, but as the shield of Italy, the scourge of the barbarians, the man who on a dawn of fire, steel, and valor, transformed fear into glory and wrote his name on the blood-soaked fields of Mediolanum with the red ink of history.

The consequences of this battle were immense.

Gallienus was celebrated as the defender of Italy and a hero of the people.

The barbarian threat to the heart of the Empire was, for a time, contained.

Moreover, this victory allowed Gallienus to consolidate his power and continue his military reforms, especially the transformation of the cavalry into the dominant force of the imperial army.

Although the Crisis of the Third Century would continue to shake the Empire for years, Mediolanum marked a turning point: a demonstration that Rome still had capable generals, disciplined armies, and the indomitable spirit that had made her great.

On the blood-stained fields before Mediolanum, where the smoke of burning wagons rose into the sky, Gallienus sealed his name in history, not as just another emperor, but as a true savior of Rome, the man who turned desperation into victory and chaos into order.

6

Battle of the Rhine River (351 AD)

In the year 351 AD, the Roman Empire was once again experiencing a period of division and turmoil.

Although the Crisis of the Third Century had passed, stability still hung by a thread.

Following the death of Constantine the Great, the Empire was divided among his sons and soon descended into civil war.

Amid this chaos, control of the frontiers—especially along the Rhine and Danube—was dangerously weakened.

The Alamanni, a powerful confederation of Germanic tribes, took advantage of this instability to cross the Rhine, plunder the wealthy provinces of Gaul, and openly challenge Roman rule.

While Emperor Constantius II was fighting the usurper Magnentius in the west, he decided to send his cousin and newly appointed Caesar, Constantius Gallus, to contain the Germanic threat and stabilize the situation along the Rhine frontier.

Constantius Gallus was young, ambitious, and still lacking notable military experience, but he had at his disposal a respectable army composed of regular units, auxiliaries, and mobile contingents of the comitatus.

His force is estimated at between 15,000 and 20,000 men, including around 10,000 legionaries and heavy infantry, about 3,000 archers and light infantry, and nearly 5,000 cavalry—among them cataphracts, light cavalry, and medium cavalry armed with lances.

Many of these troops were veterans of the civil conflict, battle-hardened and loyal to the emperor.

He also had a small logistical train, though no siege engines.

No ships were directly involved, although naval detachments patrolled the Rhine further north, guarding the river routes.

On the other side of the river, the Alamanni had assembled an imposing force, not just in numbers, but in spirit.

Their troops are estimated at no fewer than 25,000 warriors, led by several tribal chieftains, among them possibly Chnodomarius, a highly respected warlord among his people.

The Alamanni warriors were organized by clans, armed with long spears, iron swords, axes, and oval wooden shields reinforced with iron.

They fought without heavy armor but were feared for their ferocity, speed, and deep knowledge of the terrain.

They were not a professional army, but rather a tribal hammer capable of breaking undisciplined formations through massive charges and lightning ambushes.

The battle was fought near a strategic ford on the Rhine River, where the Alamanni had crossed in search of plunder and potential settlement.

Constantius Gallus, determined to prevent any further advance into the interior of Gaul, marched to intercept them.

Taking advantage of the flat terrain flanked by gentle hills and scattered woods, he deployed his army cautiously.

The Battle of the Rhine began in the tense silence that precedes a storm, as the dawn painted the gentle hills flanking the great plain by the river ford in shades of gold.

There, on the very frontier of Gaul, the fate of thousands would be decided.

Constantius Gallus, the young Caesar of the Empire, watched the horizon from his elevated position.

His face, hardened by the burden of command, showed no fear, only the steely focus of a man who knows he is about to write history with steel.

The Roman army waited in perfect formation, like a living machine.

At the center, the veteran legionaries formed a solid line of shields and spears, their helmets gleaming under the morning sun.

Behind them, ranks of Syrian archers and Balearic slingers readied their projectiles.

On the flanks, the cavalry waited like chained lions: to the right, the cataphracts, heavily armored cavalry; to the left, light horsemen and mounted archers, ready to move like the wind.

Gallus had chosen his ground well: flat, yet offering cover; open, yet with channels for surprise.

Here, he intended to turn the barbarian onslaught into a deadly trap.

The Alamanni, on the other side of the plain, made no attempt to conceal their numbers or their thirst for conquest.

They were a human tide, a horde of tribes united by the desire for plunder and blood.

More than 25,000 warriors, armed with axes, long spears, roughly forged iron swords, and wooden shields, roared like beasts beneath their tribal banners.

From the hills, the sound of drums and war horns rolled down, shaking the air.

Their leader, his name lost in the fury of battle, raised his spear to the sky and pointed toward the Roman center.

They aimed to shatter the heart of the imperial army with a single blow.

And then, like roaring thunder, the Alamanni charged.

They came down from the hills like an avalanche of flesh and iron.

The ground trembled beneath their feet.

The sky filled with howls.

The Roman line did not move.

Constantius Gallus shouted his order with a firm voice: "Hold!"

At that moment, the slings and bows began to sing.

Stones and arrows rained down on the front Germanic ranks.

Hundreds fell before they reached the line, but those who survived did so with doubled fury.

The impact was brutal.

Shields cracked, bodies slammed together, and the cries of the dying began to fill the plain.

The Roman infantry held like a wall.

The legionaries, trained to the extreme, drove their pilum into the advancing enemy and then, with a swift motion, drew their gladius to slash throats, bellies, and tendons.

The center bent, it arched, but it did not break.

On the flanks, the Gallic and Pannonian auxiliaries began to press in, pushing the Alamanni toward the center like an invisible hammer closing the trap.

Constantius Gallus, watching from his hilltop, waited.

Every second the Alamanni remained bogged down in their advance was another drop in the chalice of their defeat.

And when he saw the moment—when the Germanic charge began to lose strength, when the warriors began to trip over one another, when chaos overwhelmed their fury—he raised his hand and gave the signal.

From the right wing, the cataphracts descended at a gallop as if Ares himself were leading them.

Lances held high, helmets gleaming, their horses clad in full armor.

It was like a wave of iron roaring down, and when that wave crashed into the Germanic flank, it was as if the earth had split open.

Shields shattered, bodies pierced, entire ranks undone.

The Alamannic right wing collapsed within seconds, and simultaneously, from the eastern woods, the Roman light cavalry emerged, sweeping in like a swift shadow.

Horse archers fired without stopping, cutting through the enemy rear.

Some Alamanni tried to form a defensive circle.

Others fled.

Many ran toward the Rhine in a blind panic, but the river, cold and unforgiving, showed no mercy.

Men in heavy armor and with deep wounds were swept away by the current, their screams silenced by the waters.

The fighting continued for hours.

At the center, the legionaries advanced step by step, trampling bodies, finishing off the wounded.

Dust, smoke, and blood covered everything.

Constantius Gallus, now on foot, walked among his men, encouraging them, fighting as one of them.

By midday, the plain was silent.

The Germanic roar had been silenced.

Where there had been a tide of fury in the morning, now only corpses, blood, and fallen banners remained.

Roman casualties, though painful, were bearable: between 2,000 and 3,000 men, mostly from the infantry frontline.

But the victory was absolute.

More than 10,000 Alamanni fell on the field or during the retreat.

Thousands more were captured, chained, and sent to the provinces as slaves or political prisoners.

Several of their tribal chiefs died with swords in hand, and others were executed that same day as a warning.

The rest of the Germanic horde disintegrated.

The Rhine became a frontier once more.

Gallus had done what many thought impossible:

he had defeated a barbarian force vastly superior in number through organization, patience, and courage.

The victory was celebrated in every city of Gaul; the walls shook with joy, and the legions hailed their leader.

Constantius Gallus, until then seen merely as an administrator and noble of imperial blood, had earned his place among the great generals of Rome.

The consequences were significant. Gallus, once an obscure figure, was proclaimed by his troops as a true defender of the Empire.

Though his later reign would be marked by suspicion, repression, and tragedy, in that moment, he became a symbol of Roman resistance.

The Rhine was secured for a time, and the Alamanni, though they would attack again in later years, never forgot the slaughter they had suffered.

Emperor Constantius II, upon hearing of the victory, rewarded him with titles and power, placing growing trust in his young cousin.

On the banks of the Rhine, among bodies floating in the waters and fields stained with blood, Rome had reaffirmed its dominion.

There, where the barbarians believed the Empire was weak, the discipline, strategy, and iron will of a young general had driven them back.

7

Battle of Argentoratum (Strasbourg) (357 AD)

In the year 357 AD, the Roman Empire once again stood at a critical crossroads.

The constant pressure from the Germanic tribes along the Rhine frontier had intensified, taking advantage of years of instability and internal conflict within the Empire.

Among the most aggressive and feared tribes were the Alamanni, who for decades had crossed the Rhine in successive waves, plundering Gaul and openly challenging imperial authority.

After years of failed campaigns, devastation in the border provinces, and military humiliations, Emperor Constantius II, aware that he needed a strong commander in the West, appointed his cousin Julian, a young man, philosopher by training, and with no military experience, as Caesar of the Gallic provinces.

Many viewed him as a weak choice, but Julian proved to be not only a brilliant thinker, but also a natural strategist.

His campaign in Gaul was short, brutal, and decisive.

And his greatest achievement was forged at the Battle of Argentoratum, modern-day Strasbourg.

Julian had assembled a disciplined but relatively small army: around 13,000 to 15,000 men.

Of these, 8,000 were heavy infantry, mainly soldiers from the Gallic legions and comitatus troops hardened by years of defensive skirmishes.

He also had 2,000 archers and slingers, 1,000 light auxiliary infantry, and around 4,000 cavalry, which included the elite of the Roman mounted forces: the cataphracts, the clibanarii cavalry, and the famed squadrons of Sarmatian horse archers.

He brought no siege engines or ships, as the campaign was mobile and land-based, and the confrontation was to take place in open field.

His army, though outnumbered, was well-trained, cohesive, and high in morale after a series of small defensive victories.

On the other side, the Alamanni had crossed the Rhine with a massive horde.

Their leader was the charismatic and fierce Chnodomarius, a chieftain respected by all the western Germanic tribes.

He had succeeded in uniting the various clans to deliver a decisive blow against Rome in Gaul.

His army numbered over 30,000 men, though many were not professional soldiers, but tribal warriors driven by the thirst for plunder and the promise of land.

Armed with axes, long spears, swords, and reinforced wooden shields, and protected at most by leather or hide armor, the Alamanni were feared for their aggressiveness and their ability to overwhelm less disciplined formations.

Their strategy relied on massive charges, terror, and speed.

And this time, they planned to annihilate Julian's army in a single battle to open the way for the total conquest of Gaul.

The clash took place on the plains near Argentoratum.

Julian deployed his forces with impeccable order.

His heavy infantry formed the central core, in tight formation, with auxiliary cohorts positioned on the wings.

Behind them, he placed his archers and light infantry to provide ranged support.

On the flanks and in the rear, he stationed his heavy and medium cavalry, waiting for the right moment to strike.

Though outnumbered, his formation was solid as stone.

The Alamanni, in contrast, spread out in a wide and deep line, a human tide of shields, spears, and war cries, intending to envelop the Romans from the flanks and crush their center with sheer numbers.

The battle erupted with the fury of the old gods.

From the heights of the hills, the Alamanni descended like a living storm, a wave of wooden shields and sharpened spears, their war drums pounding through the air with a savage rhythm, like the heartbeat of death.

The ground shook beneath the advance of tens of thousands of Germanic warriors.

War horns echoed through the morning mist, and a unified, guttural, animalistic roar burst from their throats as they charged with an ancestral fury that seemed determined to devour the very heart of Rome.

Julian watched from his position, his face impassive, eyes fixed on the horizon.

He wore his purple cloak as Caesar, but bore a sword at his side and armor strapped to his chest.

He knew that morning would not be won with titles or lineage, but with blood, tactics, and resolve.

Before him, his infantry line stood firm, shields interlocked, spears ready, breath held.

The clash was like the roar of thunder tearing the sky apart.

The Roman line groaned.

The center buckled violently, retreating inch by inch under the brutal Germanic assault.

It was as if the entire world compressed into that point of impact, a cacophony of flesh, steel, splintered wood, and screams.

The Roman left, more exposed, was struck hard.

Some units began to break ranks, and for a moment, the entire flank seemed on the verge of collapse.

The Alamanni, sensing the weakness, pressed even harder, like wolves catching the scent of blood.

But then Julian did the unthinkable: he mounted his horse, seized his standard, and galloped straight into the heart of the chaos.

His personal guard followed, and the Caesar, sword in hand, plunged into the fractured line.

He did not shout orders, did not threaten, he simply raised his voice above the din with fierce calm, signaling for an immediate regrouping.

His mere presence, shining under the sun amid the blood, sweat, and dust, made the legionaries cling to their duty as if to life itself.

The flank held.

The line closed once more.

And Rome did not yield.

Meanwhile, the light infantry and Syrian archers unleashed precise volleys against the enemy flanks.

Arrows fell like dark rain upon the Germans trying to envelop the Roman positions.

The Balearic slingers, swift and agile, struck from behind the line, carving bloody gaps in the barbarian mass.

Every attempt to encircle was punished with projectiles and steel.

The Alamanni momentum began to stall.

Fury turned to doubt.

The pressure at the center was no longer a charge, but an agonizing struggle.

And then, Julian saw the moment.

From atop a small rise, he turned his horse and raised his hand.

It was the signal.

From the right flank, the cataphracts emerged, riders armored from head to stirrup, wrapped in gleaming steel, mounted on equally armored horses.

At the front rode the tribune Victor, lance raised high, and behind him the wave of iron roared and charged.

It was as if an entire wall of metal slid across the Germanic flank.

The impact was devastating, Alamannic shields splintered into a thousand pieces, bodies were hurled into the air, and cries of fury turned into screams of terror.

Simultaneously, from the left wing, the light cavalry and mounted archers launched a flanking attack.

They moved like a deadly shadow, firing without pause, cutting off all attempts at retreat.

The Germanic army, encircled, with no chance to regroup or escape, began to collapse.

Some tried to form defensive circles, others cried out to their gods as they fought hand-to-hand, knowing they would not live to see the sunset.

Julian, already covered in dust and blood, advanced on foot among his men, shouting orders, fighting, encouraging like any other soldier.

The Germanic retreat turned into a total rout.

Those who could fled toward the Rhine, but the river, generous in times of peace, was merciless that morning.

Hundreds drowned, pushed by their own or swept away by the current, trying to escape a massacre that had already become inevitable.

The waters turned red, and the fields were strewn with bodies and broken weapons.

Chnodomarius, true to his reputation, held out in the rear, fighting with ferocity.

Wounded and exhausted, he was finally surrounded and captured.

His fall shattered the last trace of Germanic resistance.

When the battle ended, the sun was already high.

The field was a wasteland of death.

Thousands of Alamanni corpses lay scattered among the few hundred Roman fallen.

The victory was absolute.

Julian, exhausted, dismounted.

He walked among his soldiers, thanking each century, praising his tribunes, acknowledging the valor of his men.

He had saved Gaul.

He had restored the Rhine frontier.

And he had proven that Rome was still capable of roaring.

The final numbers said it all: over 6,000 Alamanni killed in combat, thousands more during the retreat, and 5,000 taken prisoner.

Roman losses amounted to around 1,500 dead and twice that number wounded, but the Empire had gained far more than just a battlefield triumph.

It had regained control, pride, and most importantly: faith in itself.

The consequences of the battle were immense.

Julian, once seen as a young philosopher unfit for command, was consecrated as one of the great generals of his time.

He regained the trust of his troops, secured the Rhine frontier and restored order to a region that had been mired in chaos for years.

The Alamanni, for their part, were so severely beaten that they would not launch a major offensive against Rome for decades.

Chnodomarius was taken prisoner to Rome, where he died years later.

The victory at Argentoratum became a legend.

The philosopher Caesar had defeated the northern storm not with numbers, but with discipline, intelligence, and courage.

On the smoking fields of Strasbourg, where Roman steel cut through the barbarian avalanche, the Rhine once again roared beneath the banner of the imperial eagle.

And from that day on, no one ever doubted Julian again.

8

Battle of Carnuntum (170 AD)

In the year 170 AD, the Roman Empire was facing one of the most threatening periods since the Pax Romana established by Augustus.

Under the reign of Emperor Marcus Aurelius, the Danubian limes was under unprecedented pressure.

Amid a devastating epidemic—the Antonine Plague—the Empire's northern frontier, from the Rhine to the Danube, burned under the constant incursions of Germanic peoples who, driven by pressure from other tribes to the east, the need for land, and hunger, pushed with all their might against Rome's defenses.

Among them, the Marcomanni, a powerful Germanic tribe settled in what is now Bohemia, led a barbarian coalition that included the Quadi, Vandals, Sarmatians, and Naristi.

In a coordinated and massive offensive, the Germans crossed the frozen Danube during the harsh winter, invading the province of Pannonia, the military heart of the Danubian limes.

The fortified city of Carnuntum, one of the largest Roman strongholds along the Danube, became a crucial target.

It was home to a permanent garrison, the residence of governors, and a vital logistical hub.

Upon learning of the invasion, Emperor Marcus Aurelius, together with his co-emperor and general Lucius Verus, quickly mobilized the available forces.

The Roman army stationed in Pannonia consisted of detachments from several legions: the XIV Gemina, I Adiutrix, and elements of the X Gemina and II Italica, totaling around 25,000 to 30,000 men, including legionaries, auxiliaries, and cavalry.

Approximately 18,000 of them were heavy legionary infantry, trained and disciplined, with the rest made up of auxiliary cohorts, Syrian archers, Balearic slingers, and around 4,000 cavalrymen, including Moorish and Sarmatian cavalry in service to Rome.

Some light war machines—ballistae, scorpions, and small catapults—were mobilized for defensive use from the walls and in forward camps, but no ships were involved, as the Danube was partially frozen and the action was entirely land-based.

The Germanic force was formidable, estimated to include between 40,000 and 50,000 individuals in the coalition, many accompanied by women and children, giving the advance a migratory character.

Of these, at least 30,000 were warriors trained in tribal warfare, many armed with axes, long spears, swords, and hardened wooden shields.

Though lacking standardized armor, they were fearsome in close combat, fast and brutal.

Their leaders included King Ballomar of the Marcomanni, a seasoned warlord who had learned to avoid the mistakes of his predecessors and coordinated the attacks with precision.

The Battle of Carnuntum broke out when the Marcomanni, after several days of raiding and pillaging along the frontier, decided to lay siege to the city, believing they would find a weakened garrison.

But Marcus Aurelius, with iron discipline, had sent

reinforcements in advance.

Taking advantage of the network of military roads and the messaging system of the limes, he managed to concentrate his army just before the Germans could close the siege.

He positioned his army on the frozen plains north of Carnuntum.

He placed his legionary infantry at the center, arranged in several deep lines, with the Syrian archers and light ballistae positioned behind for support.

On the flanks, the auxiliary cavalry waited with clear orders: hold the initial blow and do not pursue until given the direct signal from the emperor.

The Germans, emboldened by their recent victories and the devastation they had wrought across Pannonia, believed themselves unstoppable.

They looked with disdain at the legions arrayed before them, thinking their shouts, sheer numbers, and fury would be enough to crush Rome once more.

They came down from the hills like an avalanche of wooden shields, crude spears, and rusted but deadly swords, roaring in unison like a living storm.

At the front were the Quadi and Naristi, wild-looking warriors, tattooed, with animal hides draped over their shoulders, advancing like an unstoppable river of muscle, hatred, and steel.

On the right flank, the Marcomanni, more disciplined and better coordinated, executed a flanking maneuver, aiming to break the Roman formation from the sides.

It was a total assault, desperate, driven by tribal pride,

yet fueled by a primal force capable of toppling empires.

The sky, clear until that moment, suddenly darkened with the flight of thousands of projectiles.

The Syrian archers and Balearic slingers tore through the air with their deadly rain, while the light ballistae and scorpions hurled iron bolts as if the gods themselves were firing lightning.

The roar of the charge mixed with the cries of the wounded, the whistle of projectiles, and the furious pounding of Germanic war drums.

The first Germanic bodies fell heavily onto the snow, but the mass kept advancing.

It was like watching a wall of flesh and rage crash into an unbreakable line of Roman shields.

The impact was thunderous.

The Roman central line shook with the collision.

The ground trembled.

Men fell instantly, pierced by spears or crushed under the weight of the Germanic push.

Roman gladii began their lethal dance, short, quick, always aiming for the abdomen, the groin, the neck.

But the pressure was immense.

Several cohorts at the center began to lose formation, pushed backward, leaving gaps that the enemy tried to exploit with savage ferocity.

It was hand-to-hand combat, knives, fists, mud, blood,

and screams.

At times, the battlefield was a hell without order, where the only law was survival.

On the Roman left flank, where Illyrian auxiliaries and Gallic troops struggled to hold their ground, the line fractured dangerously.

The Germans managed to push forward, nearly reaching the forward Roman camp.

It seemed the flank would collapse, and with it, the entire army.

But then, like a mythological figure risen from the pages of history, Marcus Aurelius, with his imperial cloak rolled up, his armor gleaming, and his sword drawn, galloped toward the broken line.

He was no philosopher in that moment, but a Roman commander forged of pure will.

At his side, the Mauri cavalry, masters of swift combat and lightning strikes, charged like bolts of thunder into the Germanic infantry that had overwhelmed the flank.

The clash was like a divine blade: the riders wheeled around the enemy, hurling javelins from afar and slashing throats in close combat.

At the same time, from the Roman right, the Sarmatian cavalry, like a wave of gleaming steel, descended in tight formation.

Their long lances and scale armor struck with such force that they tore a bloody gap into the Germanic flank.

The plan was in motion: a perfect pincer, a three-phase

maneuver of annihilation.

The enemy was being encircled, squeezed at the center, crushed from the flanks.

At that moment, Marcus Aurelius raised his hand, and the ballistae ceased firing in arcs.

They shifted their angle and aimed directly at the Germanic center, where the tribal chiefs were commanding the battle.

One by one, the bolts screamed through the air, and one struck a Quadi chieftain in the chest, bringing him down like a felled oak.

Confusion gripped the barbarian coalition. Orders ceased to arrive, and shields turned in all directions without purpose.

The momentum, which until then had seemed unstoppable, vanished like breath in the cold.

The Syrian archers advanced with lethal precision, taking elevated positions and firing at enemy groups trying to regroup.

Arrows pierced chests, collarbones, thighs, and the auxiliary cavalry finished the job.

The Germanic retreat became a chaotic rout.

Some fled toward the nearest forest, seeking the protection of the trees.

Others climbed snow-covered hills, hoping to save their lives, but the Roman light cavalry, hungry for justice, chased them down mercilessly.

There was no hiding, no mercy.

Death rode with them.

The battle lasted all day.

From the first cry at dawn to the final groan as night fell.

When the moon finally rose over the field, the ground was covered with frozen corpses.

Black blood on white snow, shields shattered like nutshells, and broken spears.

And at the center, Roman standards waving in victory, stirred by an icy wind that carried the metallic scent of blood and the smoke from fires lit for the wounded.

The Romans lost between 4,000 and 5,000 men, brave soldiers who had withstood the barbarian storm.

But the Germans were annihilated: over 15,000 dead, thousands captured, and the rest—those who managed to escape—hunted for weeks.

The tribal coalition fell apart, and Ballomar, the great chieftain, managed to flee, but he was no longer a leader, only a fugitive.

The threat to the heart of the Empire had been broken.

The victory at Carnuntum was the turning point of the First Marcomannic War.

Marcus Aurelius had contained the invasion and preserved Pannonia, the military heart of the Danube frontier.

From that point on, he began a long defensive campaign, reforming the frontier, promoting new military settlements, and reorganizing the provincial structure.

But it was also a symbolic victory:

It proved that even in times of plague, betrayal, and internal weakness, Rome still knew how to fight.

And on that frozen plain, where thousands of bodies lay beneath the snow, Rome remembered what it was: a civilization forged on the edge of the sword, guided by reason, but upheld by steel.

The Battle of Carnuntum was not just a military victory, it was an act of imperial survival.

It was Marcus Aurelius writing, in blood, the line the barbarians could not cross.

9

Battle of Vindobona (173 AD)

In the year 173 AD, during the prolonged and brutal series of conflicts known as the Marcomannic Wars, Emperor Marcus Aurelius, stoic philosopher and iron-willed commander, was immersed in a campaign of imperial survival.

After several years of Germanic invasions, betrayals, famine, and plague, the northern tribes had still not been fully subdued.

The Marcomanni and Quadi, allied in a fragile but powerful coalition, continued to harass the Danubian provinces, especially the vital region of Pannonia, whose military capital was Vindobona, modern-day Vienna.

Following the victory at Carnuntum, Marcus Aurelius had reinforced control over the limes, but the Germans continued to press forward, crossing the Danube to raid farms, besiege fortresses, and challenge Roman authority.

The emperor, who had established his headquarters near Vindobona, decided to eliminate the threat at its root.

He mobilized a combined force of legions, auxiliary troops, and cavalry drawn from several units stationed in the region.

It is estimated that his army in this operation numbered around 25,000 to 28,000 men, of which nearly 18,000 were legionaries from the XIV Gemina, X Gemina, and detachments of the II Italica.

They were joined by Gallic, Illyrian, and Dacian auxiliaries, as well as some 3,000 Syrian archers, Balearic slingers, and light infantry.

The Roman cavalry, composed of around 4,000 riders, included equites mauri, allied Sarmatian horsemen, and imperial squadrons, all under the command of experienced officers.

Mobile war machines were also deployed, such as light ballistae and scorpions mounted on carts, capable of being quickly moved to the front.

No ships were used, as the battle took place on land, south of the Danube.

The Germans, for their part, had assembled a new expeditionary force.

Although their previous defeats had reduced their numbers, the Quadi and Marcomanni had managed to regroup about 35,000 fighters, including warriors from smaller allied tribes.

Led by the Quadi king Ariogaesus and other tribal nobles, their army was poorly equipped but driven by necessity and the desire for plunder.

They carried wooden shields, long spears, curved swords, and axes, protected by thick furs or hardened leather armor.

Their strength lay in massed charges, knowledge of the terrain, and tribal fury, but they lacked the tactical discipline to match the professional Roman army.

The Battle of Vindobona began on a cold spring morning. Marcus Aurelius had arranged his forces on a plain near a bend in the Danube, with forests on both flanks and low hills to the north.

It was terrain carefully chosen: it allowed his cavalry to maneuver and hindered the enemy's mass movements.

The legionary infantry was deployed in three staggered lines, with auxiliaries on the flanks and light cavalry hidden within the woods.

The war machines were positioned in the rear, protected by infantry, ready to lash the enemy ranks.

The Germans did not wait.

Strategy was not their ally, it was fury.

Discipline was not their strength, it was the rage inherited from generations that had grown up hating the frontier, hating the order of Rome.

On the frozen plain near Vindobona, with trees still bare from winter and the Danube roaring in the distance like an ancient god who had witnessed a thousand wars, the Marcomanni roared, beat their shields with spears, and launched their charge as if they meant to tear the sky itself.

They advanced in mass, without formation, like a sea of bodies and steel.

Beside them, the Quadi, descending from the hill in a sweeping motion, hurled themselves at the Roman left flank, where Illyrian and Gallic auxiliaries held the line as best they could.

The ground shook beneath the weight of the stampede.

The sky echoed with the howls of thousands of tribal warriors.

It was a vision from another world: hair flying in the wind, bare chests, ritual tattoos, bone necklaces, and eyes lit by tribal fanaticism.

The scene seemed like the prelude to the end of the world.

But Marcus Aurelius, wrapped in his purple cloak, serene as a living marble statue, simply raised his hand from his elevated position and gave a calm order.

And then, the sky darkened, as ballistae and scorpions, lined along the rear hills and sides of the field, began their symphony of destruction.

The Syrian archers, trained to fire without pause, unleashed volleys so dense that the sun seemed to vanish for a moment.

The Balearic slingers, spinning their weapons with ancestral precision, hurled heavy projectiles that shattered skulls and collarbones.

The first Germanic line crumbled beneath that rain of death, but like a monster that feels no pain, the rest kept advancing, trampling over their fallen, determined to break the legionary line at any cost.

The clash was like the roar of a planet splitting apart.

The Roman center, formed by the XIV Gemina and II Italica, withstood the blow like a wall built of souls and steel.

The pilum, thrown just before contact, sank into flesh, pierced shields, and left bloody gaps through which death poured in.

And then the gladius, the Roman short sword, began to whirl in the hands of thousands like a scythe harvesting human wheat.

The sound was atrocious.

Bones shattered, throats were cut, groans and roars filled the air, and the tribal drums beat with a rhythm that sounded like the heartbeat of hell itself.

The Roman left flank, defended by auxiliaries, began to give way under the pressure of the Quadi.

For a moment, horror flickered in the eyes of the centurions.

The Germans broke through part of the line and began advancing toward the camp, ready to plunder, burn, and humiliate.

It was then that Marcus Aurelius, without shield, without helmet, mounted his horse and galloped toward the breach.

He said nothing.

He simply raised his sword.

And as if it were a divine signal, the mauri horsemen emerged from the forest.

Dark as night, cloaked in furs, javelins in both hands, the mauri struck in a circle, weaving in and out of the enemy line like deadly shadows.

The Quadi, caught off guard by the flanking attack, began to turn toward them.

That was their fatal mistake.

From the Roman right, the Sarmatian cavalry descended like a wave of lead and fire, gleaming scale armor, long lances, and armored horses.

The impact was devastating.

It was as if the earth had split open, and from the cracks surged horsemen of steel who struck without mercy.

The Germanic line began to unravel.

Some tried to form defensive circles; others shouted orders that no one could hear.

It was in that chaos that Marcus Aurelius ordered his third line forward, the untouched reserve of elite cohorts.

Like a second moving wall, they descended from the hill and crashed into the enemy center, planting the imperial eagles in the heart of the chaos.

At that moment, one of the Roman scorpions, swiveled on its platform, launched a bolt straight into the German center.

The projectile, with a dull whistle, tore through a Quadi chieftain, splitting him in two.

The morale of the barbarians, already wavering, collapsed.

The tribal standards fell into the mud, and the Germans tried to flee.

Some ran into the forest, others climbed the hills, seeking refuge in the mist, but the Roman light cavalry gave them no quarter.

One by one, the groups were hunted down, stabbed, captured.

The Syrian archers, still with arrows to spare, kept firing relentlessly from the heights, striking down those trying to escape along the northern flank.

The field was covered in corpses: splintered shields, broken axes, bodies still clutching useless spears.

The battle lasted the entire day.

The evening light fell over a sea of blood and smoke.

When Marcus Aurelius finally descended onto the field, he did so walking among the bodies, greeting the wounded, speaking with his centurions, calming his officers.

He did not shout victory, he only whispered: "Order has triumphed over chaos."

The Romans had lost between 3,000 and 4,000 men, many of them auxiliaries, many of them cavalry who had pursued the enemy to the farthest corners of the field.

But the Germans had been destroyed: over 15,000 dead, 5,000 captured, and the rest fleeing in chaotic retreat to the north, leaving behind their dead, their leaders, and their pride.

The tribal coalition was shattered.

The name of Ariogaesus, their king, would no longer inspire fear.

The victory at Vindobona not only secured the province of Pannonia, it also cemented Marcus Aurelius's military prestige, proving that the philosopher-emperor not only wrote about virtue and reason, but knew how to lead legions and win through blood.

The tribal coalition was broken apart, and Ariogaesus was later captured and executed.

The surviving tribes sued for peace.

10

Battle of Aquileia (238 AD)

In the turbulent year 238 AD, known as the Annus horribilis of Rome, the Empire was undergoing one of its deepest crises.

It was a time of short-lived emperors, provincial rebellions, civil wars, and borders that crumbled like sand between the fingers.

Amid this chaos, northern Italy, traditionally protected by the natural barrier of the Alps and the defensive system along the Danube, was suddenly threatened by barbarian incursions.

Taking advantage of the Empire's internal instability, a coalition of Germanic tribes—mainly Alemanni and Vandals, accompanied by contingents of Suebi and Juthungi—crossed the Julian Alps and descended into the Po Valley, plundering villas, burning farms, and spreading panic.

Their objective was clear: to reach the Adriatic and seize Aquileia, a strategic city that controlled trade routes between Italy and the Danubian provinces.

Rome, fragmented by disputes between rival emperors —Gordian III had just been elevated by the Senate after the fall of Maximinus Thrax—could not afford to lose the north.

The Senate, desperate to halt the Germanic advance, entrusted the defense of Aquileia to Generals Senecio and Balbi, who gathered an improvised but determined field army.

The Roman force consisted of between 20,000 and 22,000 men, including vexillationes from the legions of northern Italy and Pannonia (among them the II Italica and XIV Gemina), urban cohorts, Illyrian auxiliary troops, Syrian archers,

Balearic slingers, and a significant cavalry contingent—estimated at around 3,000 horsemen—composed of equites mauri, Dalmatians, and squadrons of Praetorian cavalry.

No ships were used, as the threat was entirely land-based, although some river patrols on the Natisone River supported the rear.

Light war machines—scorpiones and ballistae—were deployed, mounted on platforms within the walls of Aquileia and on campaign wagons.

The Germanic force numbered approximately 30,000 warriors, although many were not professional fighters but armed migrant bands traveling with their families, livestock, and looted goods.

Their weaponry was diverse: spears, longswords, axes, round or oval shields, and light armor made of leather or animal hide.

Their strategy was simple but effective: overwhelm with numbers, instill fear, break the lines, and advance without pause.

Their leaders included chieftains such as Gundomar and Hariulf, both known for their brutality and for coordinating fast, deadly raids.

The battle erupted on the vast plain east of Aquileia, a damp land dotted with natural canals, hidden puddles, and low woods—silent witnesses to what was about to unfold.

It was a tense, heavy morning, with fog crawling along the ground as if the earth itself were holding its breath.

The city, old and proud, watched from its walls, but its gates were closed… not to resist, but to witness how Rome would fight beyond its walls, face to face with the barbarian threat.

Senecio, a veteran of a thousand campaigns, had made a bold decision: not to fortify, not to await a siege, but to take the field, control the terrain, and cut off the head of the invasion before it reached Ravenna.

He knew the enemy.

He knew that the strength of the Germans lay in their fury, not in their discipline.

That's why his army was arranged like a living war machine, measured to the centimeter.

At the center, the legionary infantry—II Italica, XIV Gemina, and elite cohorts—formed three compact lines, hardened like an anvil of flesh.

At the front, mobile testudo units advanced in intervals, shields interlocked, ready to absorb the first impact.

On the flanks, the Illyrian and Gallic auxiliaries, swift and resilient, had clear instructions: harass, hold, feign weakness… and then encircle when the time was right.

The cavalry, a key piece of the plan, was hidden, concealed behind shrubs, low hills, and along the forest edges.

To the right, the mauri, ambushed among the trees, waited with their javelins at the ready.

To the left, the mounted Praetorians, tough, battle-hardened, silent, stood tense like a bowstring ready to be released.

Behind the center, just past the second line and protected by light infantry, the mobile ballistae and field scorpions were already aimed at the roads where the enemy was expected to arrive.

And then, like thunder over the Adriatic, the Germans came.

You heard them before you saw them, thousands of bare feet on soft earth.

War drums.

Guttural horns.

And screams, hundreds of screams, not of men, but of entire tribes crying out for blood, for plunder, for ancestral vengeance.

It was a human tide, a living roar descending in fury: Vandals and Alemanni at the front, with wooden shields and rusted axes, and Suebi sweeping down the left flank, shouting to the sky.

The Juthungi, like shadows, slithered through the trees on the right flank, waiting for their moment to strike from hiding.

Senecio, unmoving on his horse, raised his arm.

He said nothing, for he did not need to.

The ballistae roared, and a dry crack tore through the air like a burning forest splintering.

Massive bolts flew through the skies, tearing through shields and bodies alike.

With each impact, a gap opened in the barbarian formation.

From the Roman ranks, the Syrian archers and Balearic slingers unleashed a second storm.

Black arrows whistled, stones bounced off skulls, the sky turned into death.

But it wasn't enough.

The barbarians did not stop.

They advanced over the bodies of their own kin, slipped in blood, but pressed on.

The clash against the Roman center was like the collision of tectonic plates.

The legionary shields trembled but held firm, like a cliff facing the crashing tide.

The pilum flew at the last second and then, hand-to-hand combat.

Gladius against spear, shield against axe, man against man.

It was brutal, raw, without mercy, and the mud turned red.

Throats screamed until they tore.

They fought with teeth, with fists, with anything they could grasp.

The left flank, where the Gauls held position, began to give way.

The Suebi broke part of the line, and for a moment, the Roman standards faltered.

It was then that Senecio unleashed the first imperial thunder.

The praetorian cavalry, silent until then, emerged from a rise, lances lowered, in perfect formation.

They charged like a wave of iron, with the discipline of Rome and the fury of the ages.

The impact was devastating, they split the Suebi in two, cut them off from their comrades, and turned the Germanic pressure into chaos.

Panic began to spread.

Meanwhile, on the right flank, the Juthungi emerged from the forest, thinking they had taken the Romans by surprise.

But the Mauri were already waiting.

From the trees, hurling javelins at point-blank range, the African riders descended like a whirlwind, and the forest became a slaughterhouse of mud, broken leaves, and muffled screams.

The Juthungi were driven toward the center of the battlefield, just as Senecio gave his final order.

The third legionary line, fresh and untouched, composed of the elite cohorts of the XIV Gemina, advanced as a block.

It was like a wall marching into death.

In its path, the remnants of the Germanic horde were crushed.

The encirclement closed, there was no escape.

The Germans tried to flee: some ran for the forest, others threw themselves into the canals, others surrendered.

But there was no mercy.

The Roman cavalry pursued them to the last corner, and the archers, from the hills, finished off the final scattered groups.

The battlefield was covered in corpses, broken swords, fallen standards, and shields floating in the canals like ownerless leaves.

By nightfall, more than 16,000 barbarians lay dead, piled among puddles and blood.

6,000 were captured, and the rest fled toward the Alps,

pursued for days by light detachments.

The Romans had paid a high price: nearly 4,000 dead and over 5,000 wounded, many from the front lines, but the victory was absolute.

The Battle of Aquileia not only saved northern Italy but became a symbol.

In a year of murdered emperors and rebellious provinces, the Roman army had shown it still knew how to fight.

The defense of Aquileia was one of the few beacons in the chaos of 238 A.D., a lesson in resilience, strategy, and courage.

The Senate celebrated the victory as a heroic act and rewarded Senecio and Balbi with honors.

And in the city, as the bonfires burned over the enemy dead and Roman standards once again waved with pride, many thought that, even in its darkest days, Rome still roared.

BATTLES BETWEEN GERMANIC TRIBES

11

War between the Suebi and the Cherusci
(1st century A.D.)

After the Roman legions withdrew beyond the Rhine following the disaster at Teutoburg in 9 A.D., the region of free Germania was plunged into a power vacuum as vast as it was dangerous.

The Germanic tribes, who until then had found a common enemy in Rome, now turned their gaze toward one another.

Shared hatred turned into ambition, and the old tribal game of alliances, betrayals, and vengeance resurfaced with brutal force.

Among the most powerful tribes in the region were the Cherusci, led by Arminius, the great chieftain who had defeated Varus, and the Suebi, a more dispersed but equally formidable confederation, led at the time by the ambitious King Maroboduus, who, from his court in Bohemia, aspired to form a true centralized Germanic kingdom under his rule.

Arminius and Maroboduus represented two different visions of Germanic leadership: the former, charismatic and beloved by his people, was a defender of tribal independence and suspicious of absolute authority; the latter, more distant and calculating, sought to import a Roman-style monarchical structure and subjugate the other tribes under his rule.

Tensions between the two grew over the years.

Although they had been temporary allies during the rebellion against Rome, their paths diverged as soon as the Roman threat seemed to fade.

Finally, war broke out around the year 17 A.D., somewhere between the Elbe River and the eastern mountains, when Arminius summoned his allies — the Bructeri, Chauci, and Angrivarii — to confront Maroboduus and his Suebian league, which included tribes such as the Marcomanni, Quadi, and Hermunduri.

Both sides mobilized their forces on a massive scale.

It is estimated that Arminius gathered around 30,000 warriors, while Maroboduus had at least 50,000, many of them trained in Roman style after years of diplomatic contact with the Empire.

The Germanic armies were not professional, but they were hardened by years of warfare.

The soldiers were tribal warriors: they fought with long spears, iron swords, axes, simple bows, and wooden shields, protected by thick hides, rudimentary chainmail, or sometimes nothing more than paint and bravery.

Their formations were tribal, based on clans and bloodlines, and their leaders fought at the front.

The plain stretching between the Saale and Elbe rivers, crossed by clear streams and hemmed in by dense forests, became that morning an altar of war.

There, in the mist of the first rays of light, tribal banners rose, fluttering with the strength of centuries of Germanic pride.

No Roman legionary watched these lands anymore.

There was no empire to impose order, no centurions to dictate the march.

Only the cawing of crows, the crunch of branches beneath bare feet, and the increasingly close sound of Germanic war drums signaled the climax of an internal struggle for the soul of the North.

Arminius, hero of Teutoburg, knew he didn't have the luxury of brute force, as he had fewer men, fewer horses, and less heavy weaponry.

But he had something more valuable: the absolute loyalty of his clans, respect earned through blood and cunning, and an instinctive knowledge of the terrain.

He gathered his 30,000 warriors, the Cherusci in the center, divided by clans who fought shoulder to shoulder like blood brothers, the Bructeri on the left, and the Chauci, masters of forest warfare, on the right.

In the rear, behind a hill hidden by fog, his secret card awaited: a force of tribal horsemen, armed with short spears and the momentum of desperation, ready to unleash chaos at the perfect moment.

In front of him, like a dark tide of shields and spears, rose Maroboduus' army of around 50,000 men: Marcomanni, Hermunduri, Quadi, and other tribes bound under his crown.

Maroboduus was no mere tribal warlord; he was a king, and his army reflected that monarchic order imported from Rome: three well-structured corps, a powerful center that marched like a wall, and two mobile wings of cavalry and light troops that aimed to crush Arminius in a pincer movement.

Confidence ran through their ranks, for the weight of their numerical superiority was tangible, and they knew they had the power to annihilate.

The battle erupted with the first blast of the war horn, long, deep, like a cry from the forest itself.

The Marcomanni advanced like a disciplined wave, shields

interlocked, spears thrust forward, striking the ground in unison.

Each step was a drumbeat, each gaze a challenge.

From the woods, the Chauci let out war howls that echoed in response.

The Bructeri tensed like branches before a storm.

In the center, Arminius, hair braided, face painted with black lines, raised his sword and shouted to his ancestors.

The clash was brutal.

The Cherusci withstood the impact like a wall of granite.

The front lines trembled, bent, but did not break.

The clans fought shoulder to shoulder, defending not with shields but with the will to never abandon the brother at their side.

Javelins flew like swarms of hornets.

Marcomannic axes shattered shields, but the Cheruscan swords answered with surgical precision.

The mud turned red within minutes.

On the flanks, the battle took a different shape.

The Chauci set ambushes among the trees, using the forest as a living trap.

Marbod's cavalry, disoriented, ventured too far in, and the underbrush closed around them with spears from every angle.

On the other side, the Bructeri were suffering.

Without armor or reinforcements, they were being pushed back fiercely by the Quadi.

The Cheruscan left wing began to buckle, to fall back, to fracture.

Arminius saw the danger, but he did not hesitate.

He galloped forward, cutting through the center line amid the clash of battle, shouting commands, raising his standard, his figure like a wolf among wolves, and pointed to the hill.

From it, like an unleashed storm, his reserve cavalry descended, howling like beasts, lances raised high.

The Quadi, in the midst of trying to envelop the Bructeri, didn't see the charge coming.

The impact was thunderous: men and horses flew into the air, shields shattered, and Marbod's left wing disintegrated.

The entire battlefield shook.

The Bructeri, revitalized, counterattacked with fury, pressing back toward the center.

Arminius, now at the front, regrouped the Cheruscan core and launched it in a compact wedge, straight into the heart of Marbod's army.

It was the final thrust.

From the woods, the Chauci unleashed a fresh hail of javelins and arrows, now aimed at the enemy rear, where the Marcomanni were desperately trying to regroup in vain.

Marbod's men began to cry out in despair as the trap closed.

The formation unraveled.

Some warriors threw down their weapons.

Others tried to flee into the woods, but the Chauci hunted them like shadows.

Order turned to chaos, and chaos into massacre.

The entire field became a maze of corpses, blood, shattered swords, and dying screams.

The sun sank over a plain made of death.

When it was over, more than 15,000 bodies lay across the damp grass, most of them from Marbod's army.

The rest scattered in disarray.

Arminius, still bleeding from a cut on his arm, stood in the middle of the mud, his sword planted in the ground, surrounded by fallen enemy standards.

The Cherusci, the Bructeri, the Chauci... all looked to their leader knowing they had witnessed something greater than victory: the defeat of the first attempt at a Germanic monarchy.

Marbod, defeated, fled with only a small escort.

His prestige, once unquestionable, was shattered.

The tribes began to abandon him, and the coalition quickly dissolved, two years later, he was deposed by his own men.

He sought refuge in the Roman Empire, where he would die in exile, far from his forest, without a crown, without glory.

Arminius's victory cemented his prestige among the Germanic tribes, but it also sowed the seed of his downfall.

His growing power provoked jealousy among other chieftains, and years later he was assassinated by his own kin.

Even so, the war between the Suebi and the Cherusci was one of the greatest intertribal clashes of the 1st century AD, a distant echo of war without Rome, a world where the Germans chose their fate among themselves.

It was the day when tribal freedom triumphed over Germanic monarchy.

The day when the forest spoke louder than the throne.

And when the mud of the plain forever kept the wild cry of a people who still knelt before no one.

12

Battle between the Marcomanni and the Lombards (2nd century BC)

In the vast and wild territories of Germania Magna, long before Rome would dominate the region with its legions, the lands east of the Elbe and south of the Baltic were contested by countless Germanic tribes that rose and fell in endless cycles of power, revenge, and expansion.

During the 2nd century BC, in this harsh and borderless landscape, tribal rivalries were the law of the land.

And among all the tensions of the time, one rose above the rest: the conflict between the Marcomanni and the Lombards.

Both peoples shared cultural and warrior roots, but their growing power clashed in a common space: the fertile hunting and grazing lands between the Oder and Elbe rivers.

The Marcomanni, in the process of consolidating as a powerful confederation, began expanding northward under the leadership of the chieftain Tudrus, an energetic leader who sought to unite several minor tribes under his banner to form a proto-Germanic kingdom.

The Lombards, still nomadic but battle-hardened, were settling in valleys increasingly farther south, guided by King Agilmund, a young and impetuous leader determined not to allow the Marcomanni to push them out of their ancestral lands.

Tension, simmering for years through skirmishes, caravan raids, looting, and broken alliances, finally exploded.

The spark that ignited the conflict came when a Lombard

embassy was killed during a meeting with tribes allied to Tudrus.

Agilmund gathered his people, and the war drums echoed through the northern forests.

Both sides mobilized their warriors for a decisive battle over control of the region.

It is estimated that the Marcomanni assembled around 18,000 fighters, including allied clans such as the Naristi and Hermunduri.

Their strength lay in their heavy tribal infantry, warriors armed with long swords, fire-hardened wooden spears, oval shields of Roman design, and some even equipped with hardened leather armor or rudimentary chainmail obtained through trade or plunder.

On the flanks, they deployed hunters and slingers, along with a light cavalry force of about 1,000 horsemen, not trained as a formal corps, but effective in pursuit and ambushes.

The Lombards, for their part, mobilized a similar force: around 16,000 warriors, made up of light infantry with round shields, hand axes, short iron swords, and simple bows, along with about 2,000 mounted lancers.

Although they did not possess a disciplined cavalry like the Romans, they knew how to maneuver nimbly through wooded terrain.

Their warriors were more mobile, less armored, but they made up for their lack of protection with speed, ferocity, and remarkable tribal cohesion.

Agilmund relied on speed and tactical flexibility, in contrast to the frontal brutality of the Marcomanni.

The chosen battlefield was a large, uneven plain between dense forests, with several small streams, south of what is now the Oder River.

The terrain, muddy from recent rains, favored defensive movements, and neither leader was willing to give it up without a fight.

Tudrus took the initiative, deploying his army in a compact formation, with the center composed of the heavier Marcomanni and Naristi clans, while the more mobile flanks were entrusted to the Hermunduri and slingers.

In the rear, he held a small reserve of cavalry and scouts for protection.

Agilmund, for his part, opted for an open crescent-shaped formation, spreading his forces across the plain with the intent of enveloping the enemy's flanks while holding the center with more agile infantry, ready to give ground without breaking.

His mounted lancers were divided into two mobile wings, hidden behind the tree line, prepared to strike once the enemy was fully committed.

The battle began at dawn, while mist still crept among the trees and the faint light of the sun barely pierced the fog that blanketed the plain.

The silence was sepulchral, as if the forest itself held its breath, awaiting the first cry.

Then came the sound of the Marcomannic war horn, deep, long, a guttural echo that made the earth tremble.

It was the signal, and as one, Tudrus's army advanced.

Thousands of warriors, spears raised and shields locked, pounded the ground with heavy steps.

Each beat was a threat, each stride a promise of destruction.

The sound was thunderous, as if a mountain were sliding toward the enemy.

The Lombards did not move.

Silent, steady, they waited beneath the fog.

Along their line, archers drew their bows.

And when the enemy was within range, the first arrows whistled like flying shadows, slicing through the mist with a deadly song.

Some struck shields, others pierced living flesh.

The roar of the Marcomannic advance was interrupted by the first cries of the wounded.

But they did not stop.

The impact was a clash of worlds.

The Lombard center took the charge like prey beneath the blow of a bear.

Shields splintered, men hurled themselves at each other, and the mist turned red.

The Marcomanni, superior in numbers and equipment, pushed forward with the violence of a storm.

Swords shattered shields like rotted wood.

Each blow was a declaration of dominance.

Agilmund's center was retreating, bending, suffering... but it did not break.

Every step back was part of a plan.

The captains shouted orders.

The lines fell back without scattering, like a net pulled taut but refusing to snap.

Then the moment came, and Agilmund raised his sword to the sky and gave the order.

From the forests on either side of the plain, as if the trees themselves had come to life, the Lombard riders emerged.

They did not shout, they charged in silence, lances lowered, eyes locked forward.

They fell upon the Marcomannic flanks like an invisible whirlwind.

Tudrus's slingers and light troops could barely react.

The left flank disintegrated at the first impact.

Men were trampled under the feet of their own comrades.

The right flank held a little longer, but seeing itself alone, it too began to collapse.

Tudrus realized he was being encircled.

He sent in his cavalry, his horsemen charged down from the rear with roars and leveled lances.

The clash of cavalry was hellish.

Amid the mud, hooves slipped, lances shattered with a dull, violent crack.

It was a dance of steel and flesh.

But the terrain favored the Lombards, who knew every dip, every slick trap.

The Marcomannic riders, caught in a swamp of confusion, began to fall.

Agilmund saw his chance.

He ordered his light infantry on the flanks to advance and close the trap.

Like a vise clamping down on a wounded beast, the Marcomannic army was caught.

What had begun as a frontal assault became a prison of spears.

Inside, disorder reigned.

The Marcomanni fought each other for space, slipped on corpses, lost their shields, wielded knives, stones, anything that could keep them from dying.

At the heart of the battle, Tudrus kept fighting.

His sword, long and heavy, moved like a whip of death.

He cut down enemies one after another, his guard surrounding him, trying to force a path through.

But the tide was unstoppable.

There were no lines anymore, only men fighting to survive, entangled in a whirlwind of blood, mud, and smoke.

Five hours later, the sun shone high over the plain, and the fog had evaporated.

In its place were corpses, broken shields, fallen standards, and dying voices still begging for mercy.

The Marcomannic center collapsed.

Those who remained alive began to flee into the forests, abandoning their weapons, their honor, their king.

But the Lombard riders gave them no quarter.

They hunted the stragglers like hungry wolves, hurling javelins and cutting down the fugitives without mercy.

When the smoke cleared, more than 9,000 Marcomanni lay dead on the field.

At least 3,000 more were captured, many executed, others enslaved or absorbed into the victorious clans.

The Lombards, though victorious, did not emerge unscathed: around 5,000 dead and wounded, many of them fallen in the center during the early stages of the clash.

But the field was theirs.

Agilmund walked among the dead, blood covering even his face, raising his standard to the sky.

His men gathered around him, exhausted but exultant, and the chant of victory rose above the crows.

The battle between the Marcomanni and the Lombards was not merely a struggle for land.

It was the birth of a hegemony.

The victory established Agilmund as a renowned tribal leader in Germania.

The Lombards, until then a more nomadic and marginal

people, rose to a prominent position along the northern routes.

The Marcomanni, for their part, retreated southward, and Tudrus's prestige suffered a fatal blow.

His confederation was weakened for generations, losing influence to emerging tribes such as the Quadi and the Suebi.

13

Conflicts Between Vandals and Visigoths
(4th Century A.D.)

By the late 4th century A.D., the Roman world was reeling under the weight of massive migrations sweeping across Europe.

The old frontiers of the Empire no longer served as barriers, but as passageways for entire peoples fleeing hunger, the advance of the Huns, or simply searching for better lands.

In this violent crucible of movements and clashes, the Vandals —an eastern Germanic people who had descended from Scandinavia to the Danube— began moving westward, crossing Pannonia and dangerously approaching territories controlled or claimed by the Visigoths, who, after entering the Empire in 376 and their subsequent victory at Adrianople, were still struggling to settle in the rich regions of southern Gaul and northern Hispania.

At that moment, both peoples were natural enemies, not due to ancestral hatred, but because of direct competition.

They both needed the same things: land, pasture, secure routes, access to resources, and river ports.

Conflict was inevitable, and one of the fiercest erupted in the year 395 A.D., in eastern Gaul, near the confluence of the Rhône and Saône rivers, when a group of Siling and Hasding Vandals, led by the chieftain Godigisel, moved south in an attempt to seize control of a commercial and agricultural corridor that the Visigoths, under the young but relentless Alaric, considered their own.

The Vandals mobilized around 18,000 men,

including approximately 13,000 tribal infantry warriors (armed with spears, longswords, axes, and oval shields made of leather or hardened wood), 2,000 light cavalry, many of them of Sarmatian or Alanic origin, and 3,000 auxiliary family members who remained in the rear as logistical support.

Their strength lay in mobility and ferocity.

Though less organized than the Visigoths, they were hardened by years of migration and combat against other tribes, and had already sacked several minor Gallic cities.

The Visigoths, for their part, assembled a larger force: about 24,000 warriors, including an elite corps of heavy Gothic infantry with longswords, shields made of iron or reinforced wood, and partial armor composed of chainmail or layered leather.

They had around 4,000 heavy cavalry, divided between mounted nobles and mobile groups of mounted archers, along with allied auxiliary troops, especially Burgundians and Roman defectors, adding another 2,000 men.

Alaric was young but bold and meticulous.

He knew that in order to maintain the loyalty of his clans, he needed to provide land and loot, and he also knew that a defeat at the hands of the Vandals would mean losing the respect he had earned in previous campaigns.

The battle took place on a vast plain dotted with hills and small streams, west of the Rhône.

The terrain was uneven, with stretches of open pasture, wooded areas, and a northern rise that offered a strong defensive position.

Alaric chose that spot to spring his trap.

The battle began even before the sun managed to pierce the thick fog that blanketed the plain.

The silence was heavy, broken only by the distant neighing of restless horses and the metallic creak of spears being set against shields.

Atop a hill to the north of the field, Alaric, steady on his mount, watched without blinking, his plan was already in motion.

Behind him, the breeze stirred the Visigothic banners.

In the center, his heavy infantry, hardened by decades of war, formed a wall of shields and spears, each man sworn to hold the line to the end.

On both flanks, hidden among shrub-covered hills, the Visigothic heavy cavalry waited like a storm trapped in silence, ready to be unleashed.

In the rear, the mounted archers moved quietly, awaiting the signal.

And at the edges of the battlefield, like bait in a trap, the Burgundian troops feigned disarray, rehearsing the chaos meant to lure in the enemy.

To the south, through the mist, a horn sounded, a warlike roar that echoed across the plain like the earth's own lament.

Godigisel, king of the Vandals, unleashed his troops without hesitation.

First came the Alan horsemen, letting out sharp cries, descending in wedge formation.

At their backs, a wave of Vandal infantry, spread wide across the horizon, surged forward.

They were thousands strong, armed with heavy axes, long swords, rough shields, and hearts hardened by years of raiding.

The ground shook beneath their feet.

The sky darkened with dust.

The Burgundians, positioned at the edges of the battlefield, feigned panic.

They gave ground quickly, retreating toward the center, making the Vandals believe the flank was collapsing.

And they took the bait.

The enemy horsemen charged at them, trying to break through their lines.

Meanwhile, in the center, the Visigothic infantry received the blow of the Vandal tide.

The crash of impact was thunderous, splintering shields, war cries, bodies colliding.

The Visigoth line fell back slowly, like a rock pushed by the sea, but it did not break.

The spears held firm, the swords replied, it was brutal hand-to-hand combat, without pause, without mercy, without honor.

Faces covered in blood, feet sunken in the mud.

It was then that Alaric gave the signal.

From the hills on either side, the Visigothic cavalry surged forth like an avalanche of steel.

The riders, clad in scale armor and conical helmets,

descended with lances lowered, their horses draped in leather, manes stained with war.

They fell upon the Vandal flanks with primal violence.

The sound of the clash was thunderous.

The Vandal infantry, caught off guard, disintegrated within seconds.

Men dropped like stalks beneath the scythe.

Some fled, others tried to form a circle, but the Visigothic cavalry wheeled, surrounded, destroyed.

Godigisel, seeing his left flank collapse, threw all his reserves into the fight.

The central Vandal infantry hurled itself at the Visigothic center with renewed fury, desperate to break through.

The Gothic center wavered.

The lines compressed.

Every meter gained was paid for with ten bodies.

But from the higher flanks, the Visigothic mounted archers began to fire.

Showers of arrows fell upon the Vandal rear.

Precise, lethal, unrelenting.

The Vandals were trapped.

In front of them, the shield wall did not give ground.

On both sides, cavalry struck them relentlessly.

From behind, arrows tore through them.

The trap was closing.

Amid the chaos, Godigisel, his wounded arm hanging limp and blood staining his cloak, tried to rally his men.

He called them by name, pushed forward with his sword, cried out to the gods, but the line no longer existed.

A group of Visigothic riders spotted him.

They surrounded him, he fought like a cornered wolf, brought down two, but a spear pierced his side, and he fell to his knees.

One of the riders dismounted and drove a sword into his chest, and with his death, the heart of the Vandal army stopped.

What followed was a slaughter, as those still fighting threw down their weapons.

Others fled into the woods, pursued by cavalry.

The archers hunted them like animals.

The field was littered with corpses, broken standards, and spears stuck in the ground like makeshift tombstones.

The crows descended before the sun reached its zenith.

Over 12,000 Vandals died that day.

Another 4,000 were captured, many executed on the spot, others forced into slavery or conscripted into Alaric's ranks.

The Visigoths counted 6,000 dead, mostly in the center where the pressure had been unbearable, and among the Burgundians, who had feigned weakness too well and paid dearly for their role in the trap.

But the victory was crushing, and its echo spread throughout Gaul.

The roads along the Rhône fell into Visigothic hands.

Alaric, still young but now unquestioned, forged his name in blood among the Germanic powers.

No one dared challenge his right to lead again.

The victory solidified Alaric as the most feared Germanic leader in the western region.

With control over the Rhône river routes, he secured supplies, new settlements, and a strategic position for his future campaigns in Hispania and Italy.

The defeated Vandals were forced to continue their migration westward, eventually crossing the Rhine and moving into Gaul, bound for their final destination in Africa.

That day on the plain between the rivers, more than just a battle was decided.

It was the moment when the ambition of two peoples clashed without mediation, and one was left on the ground while the other rode into history.

The Visigothic victory was not only military: It was the first step in a march that would end in Rome itself.

And in the chronicles of that turbulent time, when borders melted like snow, that battle was etched as the cry of two worlds that could not share the same path.

14

Battle Between the Salian and Ripuarian Franks
(3rd Century A.D.)

In the 3rd century A.D., as the Roman Empire began to fracture under constant invasions, internal rebellions, and economic crises, a new Germanic power was rising north of the Rhine, one that would one day take Rome's place: the Franks.

Still in an early stage of tribal organization, the Franks were not a single people, but a confederation of clans divided into factions such as the Salians and the Ripuarians, each with its own chieftain, interests, and territory.

Though they shared language, blood, and common enemies, during times of imperial weakness an open rivalry arose between them: a struggle for leadership of the confederation and control over the routes of the Lower Rhine, where Roman plunder, fertile lands, and toll rights meant wealth and power.

The Salian Franks, farther west, had migrated toward what is now Brabant and the lower course of the Meuse.

They were fierce warriors, accustomed to crossing the Rhine to raid Roman villas and fight frontier garrisons.

At this time, they were led by the chieftain Malaric, an ambitious and young leader who aimed to impose his hegemony over all Franks under a single banner.

The Ripuarians, settled farther east near Cologne and the middle Rhine, were considered more "traditionalist": they maintained ties with Rome through trade and mercenary service.

Their leader was Chrocus, a veteran and respected chieftain, whose authority stemmed as much from his reputation as from his lineage.

When Malaric began demanding tribute and free passage through Ripuarian lands, and attacked several villages under Chrocus's protection, war became inevitable.

Both chieftains mobilized their clans.

The Salians assembled a force of approximately 12,000 warriors, including 8,000 infantry—spearmen, shield-bearers, and tribal swordsmen—and around 4,000 light cavalry, many of them seasoned in ambush warfare.

They lacked siege engines or fixed structures, but made up for it with speed, brutality, and strong internal cohesion.

The Ripuarians, on the other hand, managed to muster nearly 14,000 men, of whom 10,000 were infantry, many of them veterans of campaigns along the Roman limes, with more structured training, better weapons, and about 2,500 cavalry, accompanied by 1,500 auxiliaries from allied tribes such as the Bructeri.

They also had a few mobile ballistae, inherited from old Roman camps, mounted on improvised war carts, more for intimidation than precision, but useful in open terrain.

The clash took place in the wooded plains between the Meuse and the Rhine, near a strategic ford controlled by the Ripuarians.

It was summer, and the tall grass and dry soil favored cavalry mobility.

Chrocus, with a tactical mind forged through years of warfare, chose a low hill with an open plain in front and a stream to the right.

There he placed his heavy infantry in the center, in dense lines with spears at the front.

On the sides, partially hidden behind shrubs and natural formations, he positioned his cavalry, while in the rear he left the carts with the ballistae.

His Bructerian auxiliaries were stationed on the left, in a low forest, with orders to ambush any Salian maneuver.

Malaric, reckless but bold, did not shy away from battle.

He arrived from the south and formed in a wedge: his infantry was grouped into three blocks, with his best men in the center and the lighter troops on the flanks.

His cavalry was divided into two groups, flanking the ends with the intention of quickly enveloping the enemy.

His idea was clear: to break through the Ripuarian center before their orderly structure could respond.

The light of dawn had barely touched the hilltops when the first Salian horns tore through the silence.

Their roar spread like an ancestral howl, shaking the branches and scattering the birds.

Then it happened: the ground trembled with the thunder of thousands of feet.

The central Salian infantry, in wedge formation with Malaric at the head, charged forward.

The warriors hurled short axes, barbed javelins, and shouted the names of their ancestors.

The thunder of their footsteps was a living threat.

At the front, the Ripuarians stood firm.

The first line shook with the impact.

Shattered shields flew through the air.

The braided wool of the banners was soaked in blood.

It was a primitive, brutal clash, without courtesy or tactics: the center became a whirlwind of screams, mud, and steel.

Men pushed against each other like caged animals.

Some fell and were trampled by their own comrades.

For an hour, the center belonged to no one.

Every inch of ground was won and lost in pain, and every victory was the prelude to a death.

At the same time, the Salian cavalry, swift and fearsome, charged the Ripuarian flanks.

On the left wing, Chrocus's men held their ground, planting their spears like trees of iron.

But on the right, the line began to give way.

The first Ripuarian units fell back, spears splintered.

The Salians smelled blood and charged harder.

And just then, the trap closed.

From the nearby forest, the Bructeri auxiliaries, hidden in the underbrush, burst forth as if the forest itself had come to life.

Thousands of men with painted faces, curved spears, and serrated knives descended upon the right Salian flank like an avalanche of shadows.

The Salian cavalry, caught by surprise, lost cohesion in seconds.

Some tried to turn and fight, but were trapped between the Ripuarian lancers and the wild Bructeri.

It was a slaughter: the screams of the trapped Salian riders rose above the roar of battle.

In the center, seeing the balance shift, Malaric made a desperate decision.

He gathered his personal guard, the best among his warriors, men tattooed and wrapped in wolf pelts, and charged with a war cry.

His axe rose again and again, smashing shields, wounding men, opening gaps.

His attack was so fierce that, for a moment, the Ripuarian center seemed to bend.

Chrocus's banner wavered, and some thought the end had come, but Chrocus did not flinch.

From his elevated position, he raised his hand and pointed to the rear lines.

The carts with ballistae, hidden behind his formations, unleashed their fire.

The bolts cut through the sky in taut arcs, falling with terrifying whistles upon the Salian advance.

Though they didn't cause many direct deaths, the noise, the psychological shock, and the confusion sparked panic.

The Salians began looking back, and they hesitated.

And in battle, a second of hesitation is an eternity of death.

That was when the Ripuarian cavalry, freed from the right flank after the Salian collapse, maneuvered and charged the enemy center from both sides.

The wedge formation, once the Salian spearhead, became a death trap.

The Salians were surrounded on all sides, pressed from the front, struck from the flanks.

Ripuarian victory cries began to drown out the Salian roar.

Malaric, surrounded, did not retreat; with his face bloodied and one arm hanging uselessly, he fought like a man possessed.

He brought down two Ripuarian riders, threw his broken axe, and continued fighting with a short knife.

But a spear pierced his leg, and he fell.

His men tried to pull him out, forming a human shield around him, but it was too late.

The enemy cavalry overran them.

One by one they fell, and the Salian banner was thrown down, trampled in the mud.

By nightfall, the field was an open-air cemetery.

The embers of campfires lit up motionless faces,

pools of blood, and fragments of shattered shields.

The air smelled of iron, smoke, and death.

Over 7,000 Salians lay dead, dismembered, impaled, burned.

Another 2,000 were captured, chained under the impassive gaze of the Bructeri.

The Ripuarians had lost 5,000 men, many of them in the center, where bodies formed mounds of flesh, but their victory was absolute.

Chrocus dismounted, walked among the dead, and raised his people's banner with his own hands.

The riders gathered around him.

The sky was dark, but in that moment, under the stars, Frankish leadership was no longer in question.

The clans knew it, and so did the earth, soaked in blood.

The battle between Salians and Ripuarians defined internal supremacy among the Frankish people for generations.

After his victory, Chrocus was recognized as primus inter pares, the chief of the major clans, and he established a precarious balance of power that held the confederation together against external threats.

The Salians, humiliated, wandered for years without a fixed territory, until generations later, under new leaders, they would return to forge their own destiny in Roman lands.

But that battle, under the blood-red sun of the Rhine, was the moment when Frankish identity was forged in fire and spear.

15

Conflict Between the Alemanni and the Burgundians (4th Century AD)

In the 4th century AD, as the Roman Empire struggled to contain its disintegration, the regions of the middle and upper Rhine became the scene of constant disputes among Germanic peoples seeking to dominate the territories abandoned or weakened by Rome.

Among these emerging tribes stood out the Alemanni and the Burgundians, two powerful Germanic confederations that shared blood, language, and religion, but not territory.

The Alemanni, mostly settled east of the Rhine, were a warrior federation of clans without a permanent unified structure, known for their frequent raids into Gaul and their disregard for any centralized authority.

The Burgundians, on the other hand, occupied areas north of present-day Switzerland and southern Germania.

Though also a tribal society, they had begun to adopt a more hierarchical structure, with an emerging aristocracy and strong commercial ties to the Roman Empire.

Tensions between the two grew over decades.

The Alemanni, pressured by other tribes to the east, began expanding into the southern middle Rhine, seeking pastures, mines, and raiding routes.

But those territories were already claimed by the Burgundians, especially a strategic zone of hills and forests near the Neckar River, rich in iron and well-positioned to control the routes leading to the Danube.

What began as skirmishes and localized raids turned into open war when a Burgundian embassy was massacred by Alemannic clans during a falsely peaceful meeting.

Both sides summoned their forces.

The Burgundian leader, Gundomar, a seasoned chieftain, gathered approximately 18,000 warriors, including 11,000 heavy infantry armed with long swords, war axes, and reinforced wooden shields, along with 5,000 cavalry, many equipped with lances, leather armor, and conical helmets.

They also had 2,000 auxiliaries, some from allied clans such as the Turones and Semnones, as well as a small contingent of former Roman soldiers who had deserted and now served as tactical specialists.

They possessed a few minor siege engines, such as traction catapults and portable ballistae mounted on wagons.

The Alemanni, led by the fierce and young chieftain Lentomar, mobilized a horde of about 22,000 men, including 14,000 light infantry and 6,000 cavalry, many of them Alans or Sarmatian allies trained for open-field charges.

Their strength lay in speed, impact, and aggression.

In addition, around 2,000 scouts and tribal archers reinforced their rear, and they held superior knowledge of the terrain, especially the forests bordering the Neckar.

Though lacking formal discipline, their tribal cohesion and hunger for plunder made them a formidable threat.

The battle took place in a raised clearing surrounded by dense forest, east of the Neckar, during a week of fog and intermittent rain.

Gundomar chose the terrain: a wooded plateau protected

by a stream and two hills.

In the center, he deployed his infantry in a compact formation, shields interlocked and spears pointed forward, forming a defensive crescent.

On the flanks, shielded by wooded slopes, he hid his cavalry.

Behind the center, on a natural rise, he placed the mobile ballistae, which would be used to strike from a distance with heavy bolts.

On the far left, he stationed a unit of Turonian infantry to feign vulnerability and lure an enemy attack.

Lentomar arrived confident, he had seen Roman lines break before, and feared no Germanic tribe.

The dawn of the third day arrived wrapped in heavy, dense silence.

The mist drifted between the trees like a spectral army, and the cold wind swept the plain with omens of blood.

Then, without warning, the Alemannic war horns thundered with a roar so deep it made the earth tremble.

From the eastern hills, like an avalanche of fury, Lentomar's army surged into attack.

Three columns unfolded like claws: the infantry in the center, roaring with a hunger for iron, striking their shields with spears and axes; on the flanks, the light cavalry fanned out, trying to encircle the enemy, while tribal scouts, covered in furs and paint, slipped through the trees aiming to find and sever the Burgundian weak points.

The clash was immediate, harsh, and brutal.

The Burgundian infantry, stationed in the center under the command of the veteran Gundomar, formed a tight line, shields interlocked and spears like the teeth of an ancient god.

The first impact sounded like a forest cracking as it fell.

The first Alemanni fell in droves, impaled on spears or shattered by the blows of the Burgundians, but they did not retreat.

Each fallen man was replaced by another, even more furious.

It was a dark tide of shields, axes, wild hair, and burning eyes.

For over an hour, the Burgundian center held, retreating in an orderly fashion, reorganizing like a wounded serpent refusing to die.

The ground became impassable, soaked with bodies and red mud, and the air was thick with smoke, blood, and screams.

It was a hell without fire.

But on the flanks, the situation was shifting.

The Burgundian left flank, defended by Turonian and Semnon clans, began to give ground.

The Alemannic charges grew increasingly violent, and Lentomar, believing he had found the breach, ordered a full offensive on that sector, leading the charge himself.

The thunder of hooves and war cries rumbled like a storm, and for a moment, the Burgundians seemed to falter.

Then, the trap was sprung.

From the nearby trees, hidden in the mist and foliage,

the Burgundian heavy cavalry burst forth like a storm, not from one, but from both flanks.

Armed with long spears, curved swords, and shields painted with ancestral emblems, they descended like a living wall upon the Alemannic sides.

The result was devastating.

Lentomar's cavalry, trapped between its own lines and the flank assault, fell into disarray within seconds.

Men and horses collapsed upon each other as the enemy sliced through the fabric of their offensive like a blade.

The Alemannic archers and scouts, trying to respond, were struck by an unexpected blow: the Burgundian ballistae, stationed on the hill behind the center, began launching heavy bolts into the enemy rear.

It wasn't so much about accuracy as psychological impact: the whistle and crash of the projectiles sowed confusion, and the crunch of pierced bodies shattered the nerves of even the most hardened warriors.

Enraged, Lentomar launched one final charge with his personal guard, handpicked warriors, tattooed with runes, armed with double axes, sworn to die at his side.

They fell upon the Burgundian center with overwhelming violence, breaking through the front ranks, hurling men through the air like shattered dolls.

For a moment, the Burgundian line wavered, the standard shook, and the heart of the army faltered.

But then, Gundomar descended from the hill.

Clad in scale armor and a red cloak, he rode a black steed as dark as the storm.

At his side was his escort, thirty hardened men, warriors who had survived entire campaigns along the Roman limes.

Their arrival was like a lightning strike.

They charged into the tip of the Alemannic wedge, and the storm became personal.

Lentomar and Gundomar met in the heart of the chaos.

Steel against steel.

Lentomar struck down three of the escort with his axe.

He tried to cut his way to the enemy chieftain, but a Burgundian spear pierced his side.

His wounded horse fell with him.

The Alemannic leader disappeared among enemy shields, buried by his own fury, and was never seen again.

The rumor spread like wildfire: "Lentomar has fallen!"

Alemannic morale shattered in seconds.

What remained of their lines began to retreat.

First at a brisk pace, then running, and finally in absolute panic.

The Burgundian cavalry, still fresh on the flanks, pursued the fleeing enemy without mercy.

The forests echoed with hooves, screams, pleas, and the sound of swords meeting backs.

By nightfall, the field was an ocean of death.

More than 11,000 Alemanni lay dead or captured, including dozens of tribal chieftains.

Another 4,000 scattered in small bands, hunted for days.

Many minor clans abandoned Alemannic leadership and offered submission to the Burgundians.

Gundomar, wounded but standing, looked upon the fallen enemy standards and his men lighting fires over the bodies.

The Burgundians had lost nearly 6,000 men, especially in the center, where the fighting had been so close that warriors fought with fists, knives, or stones.

But the victory was not just military, it was political, symbolic, cultural.

From that day on, the Burgundians controlled the upper Rhine and were recognized as the dominant power in the region.

That battle, fought without Roman witnesses, marked the definitive rise of the Burgundians as the ruling power of the upper Rhine.

For years afterward, the Alemanni did not dare cross into their lands again.

Gundomar became a symbol of tribal unity and an undisputed leader, and in time, his successors would go on to found one of the first Germanic kingdoms recognized by Rome.

But it all began there, in the mist, the mud, and the blood, where clans faced each other and one fell so the other could rise.

It was a war of brothers, a battle without glory or witnesses, save for the crows that descended at the end.

Because the history of the Germanic peoples was forged like this: on the edge of a spear, under grey skies, where only those who could withstand the roar of war survived.

GERMANIC TRIBES AGAINST OTHER PEOPLES

16

Battle Against the Dacians (1st Century BC)

By the end of the 1st century BC, the Balkans were a mosaic of tribes, unstable alliances, and constant tensions.

On that eastern frontier of the Roman world, where the Danube marked the limits of imperial civilization, the Dacians, a Thracian people of warrior lineage, rose as the main regional power.

Ruled by chieftains such as Duras and later Decebalus, the Dacians controlled fortresses in the Carpathian Mountains and fertile valleys that provided them with wealth and manpower.

Their threat was growing ever more serious for the Romans... but also for their neighbors.

Amid that chaos, the Germanic tribes, pressing from the north and west, became entangled in a war of power and survival.

In that context, a great battle broke out in southern Dacia, not against Rome, but among the barbarian peoples themselves.

On one side, the Dacians, allied with certain Bastarnae and Sarmatian tribes, sought to secure their control over a key Danube crossing used by Germanic groups for migration and trade.

On the other, an alliance of Germanic tribes—mainly Quadi, Marcomanni, and a band of wandering Suebi—decided to act to prevent that expansion.

The result was one of the bloodiest battles of the century outside Roman control, taking place near an ancient fortified oppidum in the hills of Banat.

The Dacian and Bastarnae army numbered approximately 22,000 men, including 14,000 infantry armed with curved swords (falx), war axes, and oval shields, many wearing light armor made of hardened linen or leather.

Among them, the falxmen stood out as the most feared, capable of piercing shields with their curved blades.

They also had about 4,000 heavily armored Sarmatian cavalry, equipped with scale armor and long lances, along with 4,000 Bastarnae auxiliaries light infantry experts in guerrilla warfare, wielding slings, bows, and short knives.

Though they lacked ships and heavy siege engines, they had rudimentary catapults mounted on wagons for mobile defense.

The Germanic coalition gathered a force of approximately 26,000 men larger, but less cohesive.

The Quadi contributed around 8,000 heavy infantry armed with long spears and wide shields, along with 2,000 light cavalry.

The Marcomanni brought about 7,000 warriors, well-armed with axes and short swords, more versatile in close combat.

The Suebi, more irregular, added 6,000 men, many of them armed with agricultural tools adapted for war.

The Germanic cavalry was less disciplined, but fearsome in ambushes.

They had no siege engines, but they did use carts and improvised defensive structures.

The battle took place on a wide plateau covered in tall grass, flanked by forests and gentle hills, at the foot of a pass leading directly to the Dacian plain.

Both armies knew that whoever won there would control the routes to the south and the Danube trade.

The Dacian army, under the command of the noble Comozicus, entrenched first, forming a curved line with the center heavily defended by falxmen and the flanks protected by light Bastarnae and mounted Sarmatian units.

The Germans, led by an elderly Quadi chieftain named Hariulf, knew they had to break that formation quickly or risk being encircled.

So they deployed in a spearhead formation: the Quadi at the front, the Marcomanni on the sides, and the Suebi in the rear, ready to flank.

The dawn was pale, gray like ash, and a harsh wind swept across the plateau as if sensing the bloodshed to come.

In the thick silence of early morning, the first tribal drums were heard a deep pulse echoing through the hills, making the shields tremble.

It was the war call of the Quadi, marching in tight formation, shields raised, spears ready, their faces painted with mud and blood.

They approached like a living wall, the ground trembling under their steady march, while in the valley below, the Dacians, stationed behind a fortified line of trenches and timber, lit torches and raised their own banners covered in runes and leather.

From the central hill, the Dacian noble Comozicus watched the enemy advance with tense calm.

His falxmen, elite warriors armed with their terrible curved swords, awaited the impact.

Then, the rain fell, not from the sky, but from the arc of hundreds of Dacian bows and javelin throwers.

Bone and iron tips whistled through the air, piercing shields, thighs, and necks.

But the Quadi did not stop.

They howled, they sped up, and the clash was a collision of worlds.

The roar of impact was like a mountain cracking apart.

Shields splintered, bodies crushed against each other.

The falxmen slashed with their curved blades, tearing off arms, driving steel into flanks.

But the Quadi, hardened by decades of war on the limes, responded with savage discipline.

The center became a slaughterhouse, where the fight was not for lines or strategy, but for every breath of life.

The mud turned to blood.

The ground crunched beneath feet stepping on shattered bones.

The lines held only through mutual hatred and the will to resist.

While this unfolded, the Marcomanni, agile and swift, began their flanking maneuver.

Their leaders ordered them to advance along the sides, hurling axes and javelins in tight arcs.

The Bastarnae, allies of the Dacians, pretended to give way, retreating toward the trees.

They appeared disorganized, vulnerable.

The Germans took the bait, and that's when the ground roared.

The Sarmatian cavalry emerged like an iron nightmare.

The riders wore scale armor that gleamed through the mist.

Their lances looked like poles, and the horses, draped in leather covers, advanced like battering rams.

The charge was devastating.

The Marcomanni on the left flank were trampled before they could even lower their spears.

Men flew through the air, trampled, crushed, broken.

The Germanic wing began to collapse, and the Quadi center now felt the pressure of being flanked.

Dacian victory seemed inevitable.

But then, Hariulf, the old Quadi chieftain, gave an order that would change the course of history.

He raised his spear to the sky and shouted with a thunderous voice.

The Suebi, until then hidden in the rear, began to move.

They circled around a hill covered in shrubs, and from its summit, they descended like a horde of wolves, cloaked in black, throwing knives, roaring like a living storm.

Their target was not the front... it was the Bastarnae rear.

The impact was devastating: the Bastarnae, caught completely off guard, had no time to form up.

The Suebi fell upon them like fire, slitting throats, burning wagons, crushing the drums.

The Dacian reserves descended into chaos.

The catapults, mounted on carts, were overrun, their crews pierced by short spears.

The entire rear collapsed, and panic began to seep like poison into the front lines.

At that moment, the Quadi in the center, seeing the confusion among the enemy, redoubled their assault.

Many were dying, but they kept advancing.

The falxmen, heroic, kept fighting, but they were beginning to show signs of exhaustion.

Gaps opened, groups became isolated.

The battle turned into hand-to-hand combat, with no formations, just screams, dry heaves, and the moans of the dying.

From his hill, Comozicus watched as his army unraveled.

He tried to regroup the Sarmatians for a new charge.

But it was too late.

The Suebi were already attacking the hill, and one by one, the sentries and messengers fell.

Orders didn't get through, the horns were drowned out by the roar of battle.

Without leadership, the Sarmatian cavalry began to retreat, and with them, the Dacian spirit broke.

The line collapsed.

The falxmen died surrounded, fighting to the end.

Others threw down their weapons and fled into the forests.

The pursuit was relentless.

Quadi and Marcomannic horsemen rode down the fleeing Dacians, cutting down stragglers, burning wagons, collecting banners as trophies.

More than 13,000 Dacians, Bastarnae, and Sarmatians died that day.

Another 3,000 were captured, many of them wounded.

Some knelt and offered tribute.

Comozicus, wounded in the arm and with his helmet split, fled with barely a dozen horsemen, crossing a mountain pass to the north.

He would never regain control.

The Germans also paid their price: nearly 9,000 dead, especially among the Marcomanni on the left flank and the Quadi in the center.

But the victory was absolute.

They secured the pass, took the nearest Dacian oppidum, and gained control of the Danubian routes, establishing a hegemony that would reshape the tribal map of the region.

The consequences were profound, as Dacian prestige suffered a massive blow: their Bastarnae allies abandoned them, and several fortresses in the valleys fell under Germanic control.

The Quadi consolidated their position as the dominant force on Dacia's northern frontier, and the Suebi, thanks to their decisive action, gained land to settle in the southern foothills.

And so, in a land where empires had yet to rule, war was decided by tribal steel, ancestral fury, and instinct-forged strategy.

The tall grass of the plateau was stained red.

And for generations, the elders told how, on that day, the wolves of the north descended upon the mountains of Dacia… and won.

17

Battle Against the Celts (Gauls)
(1st Century BC)

By the mid-1st century BC, the balance of power in barbarian Europe was shifting.

As Rome expanded its presence in Gaul, the ancient tribal networks of the Gallic Celts became unstable, divided between those who sought to resist the Romans and those who wished to make peace.

Into this power vacuum, the Germanic tribes east of the Rhine, hardened by centuries of intertribal conflict, saw an opportunity.

At a moment of relative Celtic weakness, a coalition of Germans—mainly Suebi, Usipetes, and Tencteri—under the leadership of the chieftain Ariovistus, decided to cross the Rhine and conquer Gallic lands.

They weren't just seeking plunder; they sought fertile territory to settle.

Opposing them, an alliance of Gallic tribes—Arverni, Sequani, and Eburones, with support from volunteer warriors from the Nervii and Leuci—chose to stand in their way.

Although the Celts were more experienced in organized campaigns, they were divided by old rivalries and the growing shadow of Rome, which some feared even more than the Germans.

The clash took place on the plains of the upper Saône, near an important ford that controlled the routes into the interior of Gaul.

The Germanic coalition gathered approximately 30,000 men, including 22,000 infantry, well-armed with spears, long swords, round shields, and some equipped with leather or iron armor taken from Roman enemies; and 8,000 cavalry, mostly Usipetes and Tencteri, renowned for their skill in fast combat and flanking maneuvers.

They had no ships or siege engines, but they did have wagons for logistics and swift cavalry for scouting.

They were tribal warriors, bound by loyalty to their clan and the leadership of Ariovistus, who combined charisma with cruelty.

The Celtic army numbered around 35,000 men, of which 25,000 were heavy infantry, organized into tribal groups, armed with long swords, spears, and large oval shields painted with war symbols.

Some fighters wore chainmail or conical helmets, and nobles rode horses or war chariots.

They had about 6,000 cavalry and 4,000 light warriors, including slingers, archers, and javelin throwers.

Their leaders included the Arvernian Casticos, a veteran of internal conflicts, and the young and fiery Sequani Segovax.

Though more numerous, the Gauls were less disciplined as a unified army.

The battlefield was an open plain, bordered by low forests and a narrow river, which limited maneuverability.

Ariovistus chose slightly elevated ground with his right flank protected by a grove and his left open for cavalry deployment.

He arranged his infantry in a compact formation, with the Suebi in the center, flanked by the Tencteri and Usipetes.

The cavalry was divided: half hidden behind the grove for a surprise attack, the other ready to flank in open ground.

The Gauls formed a large frontal line, with the Arverni and Eburones at the center, the Nervii on the right flank, and the Leuci on the left.

The war chariots and mounted nobles were positioned behind the infantry to intervene where needed.

The slingers and javelin throwers were deployed at the front, in the vanguard.

The dawn mist slowly rose over the plain, filtering the light through the trees like a promise of blood.

Then the Celtic drums began to roar.

It wasn't music: it was the heartbeat of a people on the edge of war.

Along the Gallic line, warriors struck their shields with spears, painted in blue, adorned with iron torcs and ancient cries.

In front of them, the Germans waited in silence, like stones in the river, unmoved, until the first whistle cut through the air.

The Gallic javelin throwers surged forward, running through the mist with precision and fury.

Their projectiles rained down on the German lines, bouncing off shields, piercing arms, legs, and sides.

Some Suebi fell, crying out in incomprehensible dialects.

But they did not retreat.

Then, in an explosion of raw sound, the Germans responded with a single war cry, a savage howl that seemed to rise from the earth itself, guttural and deep, as if the land were screaming.

And then they charged.

The Germanic infantry, with round shields, spears forward, and eyes bloodshot with rage, advanced like a wave of iron, striking the ground with each step as if marking the countdown to fate.

The impact against the Gallic line was an eruption of chaos: splintered wood, broken bones, screams, blood in the air.

The Gallic center, made up of Arverni and Eburones, trembled like a cracking dam.

For over an hour, the battle at the center was a shapeless hell, where men no longer fought for banner or tribe, but to breathe one more minute.

The Suebi, tall, muscular, covered in furs and mud, fought like beasts, driving spears, tearing throats, pushing with shoulders and fury.

The Eburones, brave but overwhelmed, began to break.

Small cracks opened in the line.

Bodies formed mounds between the ranks.

The mud turned red.

Seeing the danger, Segovax—young, impulsive, heroic—ordered his cavalry to charge the German left flank.

It was a magnificent sight: hundreds of Gallic horsemen descending with lowered lances, horses draped in embroidered cloth, and horns echoing across the plain.

But Ariovistus had foreseen the move, and from the forest, like a swarm of wolves—the Usipete cavalry emerged.

The ambushed Germanic riders hurled themselves at the Gallic rear with inhuman fury.

Caught between two fronts, the Celtic horsemen were surrounded, crushed, annihilated.

Some surrendered, but most were struck down and trampled by their own horses.

The Gallic banners sank into the mud, and with them, the hope of their left flank.

On the other wing, the Nervii held firm like a stone wall.

But when they saw the collapse of their kin, when the Usipetes began to flank them, their confidence wavered.

One by one, the clans began to scatter, no orders, no commanding voice.

What had been a line turned into a wave of desperate men.

The center, however, still held.

Amid the chaos, Casticos, the Arvernian noble, continued to fight.

Standing atop his war chariot, wielding a longsword like a torch of justice, he cut down enemies like a tribal god.

Each strike was a prayer, but not even legend can defy time.

When the Suebi broke through the second line, they surrounded him.

One of them—it is said to have been Ariovistus's son—threw

his spear with such force that it pierced the Arvernian's shield and chest.

Casticos fell from his chariot like a felled oak, and the ground seemed to tremble with his death.

The Gauls saw him fall, and with him, their spirit fell.

Many dropped their weapons, and others shouted the names of their ancestors and fled.

The Germanic cavalry followed them like wolves on the hunt, cutting them down without mercy, without pause.

Those who ran were struck down by spears.

Those who hid were dragged from the bushes by blades, and the forests burned with screams and death.

More than 20,000 Gauls died that day.

The Saône River ran red.

Another 6,000 were captured, chained, marked, turned into currency for trade.

The Germans left 7,000 bodies on the field, but they departed with victory in their hands, the land beneath their feet, and the future on their spears.

The battle shifted the balance in Gaul, as Ariovistus and his people occupied the conquered territory, establishing a stable base west of the Rhine.

Several Gallic clans swore obedience to avoid destruction.

Rome, alarmed, would begin to intervene shortly after: the shadow of Caesar was approaching.

But in that moment, on that blood-stained plain, the Germans had crossed the Rhine not as invaders, but as conquerors.

18

Battle Against the Sarmatians (2nd Century AD)

By the mid-2nd century AD, while the Roman Empire was waging wars on multiple fronts, a different kind of conflict was brewing north of the Danube, beyond the reach of imperial eyes.

In the vast, wind-swept steppes of the middle Danube, two worlds were about to collide.

On one side, the Germanic tribes of the Marcomanni and Quadi, recently reinforced after their clashes with Rome; on the other, the hosts of the Sarmatians, kings of the plains, horse-riding nomads feared for their speed, ferocity, and armored heavy cavalry.

The conflict began when Sarmatian bands, pressured by hostile movements in the Black Sea region and by famine, started to push into territories traditionally controlled by the Marcomanni and Quadi in the regions north of Pannonia.

What began as border skirmishes between scouts turned into open war when a group of Quadi nobles was killed in an ambush during peace negotiations.

Tired of the raids, the Germanic clans formed an alliance.

The Marcomannic chieftain Baeloric and the Quadi king Sinthar, both veterans of conflicts with Rome, joined forces to confront the threat from the steppe.

The Sarmatians, for their part, were led by the noble Izarxas, a commander respected for his ruthless strategy and his control over the Roxolani and Iazyges clans.

The forces gathered were enormous for a tribal conflict.

The Marcomanni and Quadi assembled approximately 28,000 men, including 18,000 infantry armed with long spears, axes, Germanic swords, and oval shields, organized into compact tribal phalanxes.

Many wore leather armor, and some chieftains used looted Roman gear.

Their cavalry was smaller but effective: about 4,000 riders, divided between scouts and mounted nobles.

They also had 6,000 auxiliary warriors, including wandering Suebi and former Sarmatian deserters familiar with the terrain and cavalry tactics.

They had no ships or siege engines, but they did possess defensive wagons and a few light traction ballistae mounted on improvised structures.

The Sarmatians fielded a slightly smaller force in numbers but formidable in mobility and shock power: around 24,000 men, the majority of them cavalry, about 16,000 heavy Sarmatian horsemen clad in scale or plate armor, armed with long thrusting lances (kontos) and curved swords; and 8,000 auxiliary light cavalry, mounted archers of nomadic lineage who could unleash wave after wave of arrows while riding.

The Sarmatians did not use regular infantry, but they carried logistical wagons, tribal standards decorated with horsehair, and a level of military discipline far superior to that of most barbarian peoples of their time.

The clash took place near a large meander of the Danube, on a vast plain crisscrossed by streams and patches of tall grass.

Baeloric and Sinthar chose an area where they could form a semi-static defense, with the right flank protected by a line of gentle hills and the left open for the deployment of their light cavalry.

They formed three lines of infantry, alternating Marcomanni and Quadi warriors, with stakes and improvised trenches in front.

The cavalry was split between the flanks and a mobile reserve at the center.

The ballistae were mounted on reinforced wagons positioned behind the infantry.

The morning mist hung low and heavy over the Danube plain, as if the earth were holding its breath.

Then, from the east, came the roar: Izarxas did not wait.

Dawn erupted in shouts and hoofbeats as the first Sarmatian units emerged like a storm of steel, their bows gleaming, horses draped in leather covers, and standards whipping like serpents in the wind.

Their light cavalry circled, unleashing waves of deadly arrows.

The Germanic line, still forming under the gray light, raised their shields like a living wall, receiving the projectiles with cracks and cries.

Men fell pierced through, others crouched low, but none retreated.

The Sarmatian riders did not relent: they galloped, fired, turned, vanished into the mist, and reappeared again.

Moments later, the fog was torn apart by the roar of the main charge.

The Sarmatian heavy cavalry, the most feared warriors of the steppes, were now advancing in wedge formation, thousands of riders clad in scale armor, with lances as long as banners and helmets adorned with black horsehair plumes.

The ground trembled beneath their advance, a wave of iron with a thunderous heart.

The Germans did not flinch.

They drove stakes into the ground, reinforced their lines, lowered their spears, and locked their shields tight.

The war cries of the Suebi and Marcomanni rose to drown out fear.

Then, the impact was brutal, a collision of civilizations.

The first Sarmatian squadrons pierced the central line like blades, lances shattering bones, helmets flying, men torn from their feet like leaves in a hurricane.

But the Germans did not give way.

At every breach, a warrior stepped in.

At every gap, the dead were replaced by fury.

On the left flank, Sinthar unleashed his Quadi cavalry, battle-hardened men armed with war axes, who crashed into the flanks of the Sarmatian riders with fierce intensity.

At the same time, the Suebi auxiliaries, hidden along the edge of the nearby forest, began harassing the enemy's sides with guerrilla tactics, hurling javelins and attacking in short, bloody waves.

In the center, Baeloric reorganized the second line with what remained of his heavy infantry, while the ballistae mounted on wagons launched bolts as heavy as the spears of the gods, bringing down horses and riders with every strike.

The battle became a vortex of steel and mud.

Men screamed without knowing if it was victory or death.

The fighting was so close that the breath of the enemy burned the face.

Broken spears were replaced with knives, shields were used as battering rams.

In the Germanic rear, a group of Sarmatians infiltrated through a dry streambed and attacked the supply wagons, causing momentary confusion.

But Sinthar's personal guard responded, swords drawn, and the Quadi king himself fought on foot, killing three riders with his own hands before being wounded in the leg.

The sun began to sink, and the plain looked like a cursed field.

The bodies of men and horses covered the ground.

The weapons were red.

The banners barely fluttered.

Then Baeloric saw what he had been waiting for:
the Sarmatian right flank was beginning to stretch, losing cohesion.

They were tired, their momentum fading, this was the moment.

With a shout that seemed to tear through the mist, Baeloric launched his final offensive.

His entire reserve—cavalry, slingers, fresh infantry—

descended from the hill like an unstoppable wave.

They struck the Sarmatian rear with such fury that the line broke in seconds.

Izarxas's riders, surrounded and disorganized, began to retreat.

What started as a retreat turned into a rout, and then a rout into full-blown panic.

Izarxas tried to regroup, sword in hand, shouting orders from horseback.

But a Quadi spear pierced the side of his horse, and both went down.

Wounded, covered in mud and blood, he tried to rise, but when his own men saw him fall, they lost all hope.

The Sarmatian army collapsed.

What followed was a hunt.

The Germanic riders, despite their exhaustion, pursued the Sarmatians for hours.

The nearby forests echoed with screams.

Some enemy riders surrendered, others hid, but most were cut down without mercy.

Bonfire after bonfire was lit over the bodies.

The sky turned red, as if the earth itself were bleeding.

When night fell, the plain was a nameless graveyard.

Nearly 12,000 Sarmatians died that day, among them dozens

of nobles, clan chiefs, and renowned warriors.

Another 5,000 were captured, chained, stripped of their horses, and paraded as trophies.

The rest fled east, crossing the Tisza, bearing the scars of defeat.

The Germans also paid a heavy price: around 9,000 dead, especially in the center, where the Sarmatian charge had been unstoppable.

But their victory was complete.

The threat from the steppes had been silenced.

After the battle, Sarmatian influence over the middle Danube was broken for decades.

The Marcomanni and Quadi consolidated their hegemony in the region, and some Sarmatian clans sued for peace and were assimilated.

Mounds were raised for the fallen, and the epic songs of Baeloric and Sinthar became part of the tribal soul of their people.

19

Clash Against the Scythians (3rd Century BC)

By the mid-3rd century BC, before Rome dominated the Danube basin and centuries before the Goths threatened the Empire, the eastern Germanic peoples, especially the Bastarnae, early Goths, and Rugian and Scirian clans, were expanding southeastward.

Driven by population growth and pressure from other clans, these peoples began descending into the fertile plains and valleys of the Black Sea, coming into direct contact with a very different world: that of the Scythians, the nomadic horsemen of the East, lords of the steppe, heirs to centuries of mounted warrior tradition.

At first, relations were commercial, involving the exchange of amber, livestock, iron, and grain.

But tensions over control of pasturelands, trade routes, and tribute soon escalated into conflict.

The eastern Germans, led by the Bastarnae chieftain Rugomar, gathered a coalition of clans with the goal of securing permanent settlements near the mouths of the Dniester.

They assembled an estimated army of 25,000 men, of which 17,000 were infantry: tribal warriors armed with long spears, battle axes, iron swords, and round or oval shields, many wearing leather or bronze helmets looted from Greek merchants.

Their cavalry numbered around 6,000 riders, including Bastarnae and Rugian warriors mounted and heavily armed, using tactics inspired by earlier battles with the Thracians.

They also had around 2,000 archers and slingers recruited from subordinate tribes.

They had no ships in the area nor siege engines, but they did possess logistical wagons and a small elite mounted guard that accompanied Rugomar.

The Scythians, alerted by these incursions, responded under the command of King Skiluros, a veteran and feared chieftain known for his brutality and mastery of mobile warfare.

His army, smaller in number but extremely mobile, consisted of around 21,000 fighters, almost all of them cavalry, 12,000 mounted archers equipped with Scythian composite bows, capable of shooting accurately at full gallop, and 9,000 mounted lancers, some clad in hardened leather or scale armor, armed with curved swords and whips.

They did not use infantry except to defend their camps, and they had no siege engines or fixed fortifications.

Their tactic was simple but devastating: harass, isolate, encircle, and destroy.

The battle took place on the open plain of the lower Bug, near the marshy shores of the Black Sea.

It was an endless expanse of rolling grass and low shrubs, perfect for cavalry.

Rugomar knew this, but he had positioned his army on high ground, on a natural plateau surrounded by small ravines.

There, he deployed his infantry in a semicircular formation, with shields forming a tight line, and the flanks protected by Bastarnae cavalry.

In the rear, he placed his slingers and archers, along with his personal guard.

His intention was to withstand the first blow, wear down the enemy riders, and then launch a full charge to break the Scythian line.

The Scythians arrived at dawn, as if the sunrise itself rode beside them.

The horizon was filled with dark mounted figures, wrapped in furs, with banners whipping like snakes in the wind.

The dust of the gallop mixed with the shrill neighing of thousands of horses.

And atop a hill, with eyes like frozen steel, Skiluros raised his arm and gave the signal without uttering a single word.

The battle began with the song of bowstrings.

The mounted Scythian archers spread out into three wings and began circling the plateau like vultures over wounded prey.

They fired while galloping, retreating without breaking rhythm, unleashing arrows with unnatural precision.

The first volleys were devastating: the projectiles rained down like swarms of wasps, piercing shields, embedding in arms, legs, and faces.

The crack of splintering wood blended with the screams of the wounded.

The Germans held their ground, shields raised, teeth clenched, not taking a single step back.

Rugomar, standing tall among his men, did not move.

He waited for the exact moment, like a hunter who knows his prey.

But the Scythians were armed wind.

They offered no clear target.

They circled, pulled back, feigned retreats, then reappeared like specters in the dust.

One feint turned into a real charge: from the right flank, a group of Scythian lancers hurled themselves forward with fury.

Their long spears struck the Germanic ranks like hooks.

Some Germans were thrown into the air, and the right wing wavered.

Without losing a second, Rugomar ordered his Bastarnae cavalry to counterattack.

The sound of the clash was deafening: the pounding of hooves, metal against bone, the screams of men falling under hooves and blades.

There began the whirlwind of the flanks: a chaotic struggle of man against man, where order vanished, and all that remained was confusion, gasps, neighs, and the brutal force of survival.

At the same time, the Scythian archers continued to rain death from afar.

Every Germanic attempt to advance was stopped by a storm of arrows.

Many died without ever swinging their weapons, their eyes wide open, not understanding where the final blow had come from.

Rugomar saw then that his men were dying without a fight.

The pressure was unbearable.

He shouted orders and blew the aurochs horn hanging from his waist.

And at last, he unleashed the soul of his army: the Germanic infantry descended from the hill with a roar that shook the earth.

Thousands of men, armed with spears, axes, and tribal fury, charged down like an avalanche.

It was their moment.

They caught several Scythian groups by surprise, those who hadn't withdrawn in time.

They reached them and tore them apart without mercy.

Spears pierced necks, shields struck like battering rams, axes came down like scythes.

Scythian blood finally mixed with the earth, but Skiluros had foreseen that reaction.

Atop a hill, hidden behind a small grove of willows, an entire unit of Scythian lancers waited for the signal.

When the Germanic center stretched too far, they struck like lightning at the now-vulnerable left flank.

It was a slaughter.

At the same time, the mounted archers adjusted their angle and began firing diagonally, hitting the very heart of the enemy formation.

The Germanic left collapsed within minutes.

The lines broke like thin ice.

The Scythian riders began to encircle from both sides.

What had been a front turned into a trap.

Rugomar shouted, sword raised, trying to rally his men.

But his personal guard was wiped out one by one.

He himself fell from his horse, a spear in his side, covered in blood, dragged through the mud.

Some Germans resisted to the end, forming small clusters, back to back, surrounded, fighting with knives and fists.

Others tried to form a shield circle, but the Scythians' mobility overwhelmed them completely.

The riders allowed no respite: they cut off escape routes, set supply wagons ablaze, and fired every last arrow.

The field became a hunting ground.

Rugomar was captured, lifeless, exhausted, covered in wounds.

He was brought before Skiluros, who dismounted with the calm of a cruel god.

Without trial, without a word, he slit his throat with his own curved sword and left him to the vultures.

When night fell, the plain was a sea of lifeless bodies.

More than 15,000 Germans lay dead, many unrecognizable.

Another 4,000 were captured, dragged away with ropes around their necks, condemned to slavery.

The Scythians had lost around 3,000 men, mostly in the flank battles, but their victory was total and crushing.

For days, campfires burned.

Germanic banners were set ablaze.

Sacrifices were offered to the gods of the steppe.

After the battle, the Germanic tribes withdrew northward.

Their expansion toward the Black Sea was halted for decades.

The Scythians consolidated their control over the coastal routes and demanded tribute from neighboring peoples, along with captured slaves and livestock.

For the Germans, it was a bloody lesson.

For the Scythians, it was an affirmation of supremacy.

The plains of the Bug never forgot that day, and the crows cawed for weeks over the remains of a shattered dream.

20

Battle of the Moselle River (388 AD)

By the late 4th century AD, the Roman Empire found itself at a critical crossroads.

After the death of Emperor Theodosius I in 395, the empire was divided between his sons: Arcadius ruled in the East and Honorius in the West.

This fragmentation weakened central authority, leaving the western frontiers vulnerable to incursions by various peoples.

In this context, the Franks, a confederation of Germanic tribes settled along the Rhine River, emerged as both allies and, at times, adversaries of Rome.

At the same time, the Huns, a nomadic people originating from the steppes of Central Asia, burst into Europe, displacing other tribes and sowing chaos in the border regions.

Their arrival triggered a wave of migrations and conflicts that further destabilized the already fragile balance of power in the region.

In the year 388 AD, near the Moselle River, a significant confrontation took place between the Franks and a coalition of Huns and other eastern tribes seeking to expand their influence westward.

The Frankish army was composed of approximately 12,000 warriors, with infantry forming the core, equipped with spears, shields, and short swords, trained to fight in tight formations.

The cavalry, though smaller in number, played a crucial role in fast maneuvers and flanking attacks.

Leading the Frankish forces was King Clodion, a shrewd and courageous leader known for his ability to unite the various tribes under a common cause.

On the other side, the coalition of Huns and allied tribes numbered around 15,000 fighters.

The Huns were famous for their light cavalry, mounted archers who could shoot with deadly precision while galloping at high speed.

Their allies, which included Ostrogoths and Alans, contributed both infantry and heavy cavalry, creating a versatile and formidable army.

The Hunnic leader, Uldin, was known for his ferocity in battle and his talent for forging strategic alliances.

The dawn over the Moselle Valley brought not light, but fog.

A thick, low fog that crept like a gray veil between the trees and gentle hills, concealing the enemy and holding the breath of thousands of men who knew that day would be remembered for centuries.

From the hill where they waited, the Frankish warriors could barely make out dark shapes moving in the distance.

The horses neighed uneasily, shields thudded against the ground, and whispers and prayers mingled with the mist.

And then, as if the wind had shifted, the silence was shattered by a thunderous roar: the wild gallop of death.

The Huns had arrived.

From the fog, the shadow of the Hunnic-Alan cavalry emerged like lightning.

Thousands of light horsemen, with short bows and raised spears, came thundering down at full speed upon the Frankish right flank.

Clodion's warriors barely had time to raise their shields.

The charge was lightning-fast, a bolt that tore through the mist and struck them like a storm.

The first Huns crashed into the spears and shields, many impaled, some thrown by the momentum of their horses.

But the weight of the mass, the speed, and the fury of the charge forced the Franks back.

The line bent, creaked, seemed on the verge of breaking.

And then, behind the Hunnic riders, the Ostrogoths emerged.

Heavy, armored, ferocious.

Their heavy cavalry stormed into the assault like an iron battering ram, adding brutal force to the initial blow.

The hillside trembled under their hooves.

Their guttural cries rose above the din.

The Frankish right wing gave ground, step by step, pushed by an avalanche of flesh, steel, and fury.

But Clodion was not a king who yielded to the charge.

From the top of the hill, he ordered his cavalry to ambush the enemy flank.

While his infantry held on with clenched teeth, the Frankish riders, hidden behind a small grove and familiar with the terrain, descended at full speed down a side slope.

Like wolves upon an unsuspecting herd, they struck the rear of the Hunnic mounted archers.

The attack was devastating.

The surprise, total.

Many Huns barely had time to turn before being pierced by Frankish spears.

The Hunnic lines fell into disarray.

Confusion spread like dry fire.

What had been a coordinated assault turned into bloody chaos.

The fog still covered the valley, but now it was soaked with screams, the clash of metal, and the agonized neighing of dying horses.

Clodion, with his great red-painted shield and bare sword, rode into the heart of the fray.

He fought with the fury of a war god, shouting commands, wielding his blade with savage precision, his very presence breathing strength into his exhausted men.

On the other side of the field, the Hunnic warlord Uldin, mounted on his black steed, led his troops through the dust and fog.

His shouts and signals tried to restore cohesion to an army that was falling apart by the minute.

The Ostrogoths, disciplined, attempted to regroup, while the Huns, disoriented by the rear attack, struggled to regain the initiative.

Hours passed in relentless hell.

Bodies piled up, the mud mixed with blood.

Broken spears became improvised stakes, and warriors fought with daggers, stones, or their bare fists.

The fog slowly lifted, like a curtain revealing a nightmare scene: thousands of dead, wounded crying for help, broken banners, and riderless horses wandering among the corpses.

The attrition was unbearable.

The lines had devolved into a tangled mass of individual combat.

By late afternoon, with the sun sinking behind the hills, Uldin realized he could no longer break the Frankish wall.

His riders were exhausted, his archers scattered, the Ostrogoths decimated.

If he stayed a moment longer, the defeat would be total.

With a bitter gesture, he ordered the retreat.

The Huns and their allies pulled back at full speed, pursued by the Frankish cavalry, who harassed them until darkness covered the field.

Clodion's warriors, exhausted, had no strength left for a long pursuit.

When the moon rose over the Moselle, only silence and death remained.

The losses were terrible. More than 5,000 Franks lay dead or dying.

The Hunnic-Ostrogothic coalition had left 6,000 corpses among the reeds and mud.

The plain smelled of blood, smoke, and sweat.

Clodion, though victorious, understood the high cost of the battle and ordered the wounded to be tended and tribute paid to the fallen.

The victory at the Moselle River solidified the Franks' position in the region and demonstrated their ability to face and repel the feared Hunnic hordes.

However, the heavy losses temporarily weakened their military strength, preventing immediate expansion.

As for the Huns, though defeated, they remained a threat on other Roman frontiers.

This battle, though not decisive in strategic terms, symbolized the fierce resistance of the Germanic peoples against eastern invasions and became a legend passed down through generations among the Franks.

Printed in Dunstable, United Kingdom